WEIGHTLIFTING FOR BEGINNERS

WEIGHTLIFTING FOR BEGINNERS

DAN KENT
MIHAI IVAN

Edited by THOMAS WILLIAM LAMBIE
Additional Photographs BOBBIE ROSS
Technical Reviewer MARIUS HARDIMAN
Proofreader ROGER DALLIARD

Powerful Ideas Press
Books about strength sports

Powerful Ideas Press

1 Watts Road, Studley, B80 7PT, United Kingdom

www.powerful-ideas-press.com

❀ Created with Vellum

For Helen and Laura.
You make us better people.

CONTENTS

PART 6
DISCIPLINE

FOREWORD

MIHAI IVAN

Before you begin reading this book, I want you to do a quick imagination exercise. In weightlifting competitions, you have a total of six attempts, one minute for each – three for snatch and three for clean and jerk. If you don't know yet what these words mean, don't worry, you'll find out in the following pages. For now, just stick to imagining that all the hard work you've put into your training for months, maybe years, will be shown off in just six minutes.

Let's take it even a little further. You have prepared for the Olympics your whole career and this competition is the pinnacle of your achievements so far. You are there now, waiting to take your final turn on the lifting platform. You have one last attempt: if you make a good lift, this can bring you a gold medal; if it is a no lift, you're off the podium completely. How do you approach this? What do you tell yourself in those moments? Any fear of failure creeping in? Will you go for all or nothing? How badly do you want this? Your whole career as an athlete brought you up to this decisive point ... You hear the buzzer ... thirty seconds to go ... What do you do?

Back to reality. It's a long, long way to the Olympics, and many people who start weightlifting don't even start competing. In its essence, weightlifting is a constant competition with yourself. It's you, striving to become better and better with each lift. And it will profoundly change you in the process, both physically and mentally.

This book comes as deep act of gratitude towards the weightlifting world for the chance I got when I was just fourteen years old, when I started.

The context in which I used to live in at that time was far from sunshine and rainbows, even further from merely healthy for a teenager's development. I then discovered the wonderful sport of weightlifting, which became my safe space, a refuge in which I could work with my negative feelings and frustrations. With time, I came to realise that weightlifting is not about lifting and throwing around weights with frustration, but about work, focus, and self-development. This sport taught me the importance of having a greater purpose that drives you, breaking it down into smaller and more achievable goals and turning these into a plan that keeps you motivated and gives you constant satisfaction.

This way of 'planning' seamlessly transferred to the way I approach life and it helped me in everything I've achieved so far, both on a professional and personal level.

Whether you will be competing in any form or just doing it as hobby in your backyard, I wish for you to discover the capacity that this sport has to bring out the best in you, while setting you up for a rendezvous with your greatest fears. It's a constant learning process. When you're about to lift, there are a few split seconds in which education, social status, what you ate last night or what you wear today at work don't matter. It's just you and your bar, all your resources focused towards it.

If you go on to compete, things will get more interesting. It becomes a game of chess. You can play in defence (lifting with the hope that your opponent won't make it), you can play offence (always the last to lift a bar, to 'have the last say'), or you can bluff (pushing your opponent towards failure). Regardless of your approach, all your hard work and dedication are demonstrated in those six minutes on the competition lifting platform.

This book is a way for me to pass on the knowledge I've gathered in more than a decade as a professional weightlifter and coach. My deep gratitude goes to my coaches from Romania, Adrian Ionescu and Doru Agache, who shaped me into the athlete, and then the coach that I've become. I have also to thank Sam Dovey, my UK coach, for the wonderful context in which I could pursue my passion. My special thanks go to Dan Kent, for coaching, support and the opportunities he has provided me with, including the chance to contribute to this book, and to Helen Kent, the person who believed in me even when I didn't. Last but not least, I wish to thank all the opponents I have ever encountered in competitions, for they have taught me both to win and lose with grace.

As you study this book, I want you to discover a sport, a lifestyle and a healthy way of thinking. I always say that out of a million athletes, only a few will grow into world-renowned champions, but all will grow into beautiful human beings.

DAN KENT

I think Mihai has perfectly summed up why Olympic weightlifting can be more than a sport to those who take part in it. Regrettably, I came to the sport too late to really excel (although I still do my best as a masters lifter!) but I gain a huge amount from my own struggle to hit new personal bests. I also take great satisfaction in supporting more talented lifters than me in their successes. I have been very lucky to work with some fantastic athletes, whether they are youth, seniors or masters lifters, and to experience moments that will stay with me forever.

Of course, along with joyful moments of success, there are also times when things don't go to plan and when progress is hard. While tough at the time, looking back it becomes obvious that these periods are just as important. Overcoming adversity and disappointment teaches many lessons.

I would like to thank all of the members of KBT Weightlifting Club (now Warwickshire Weightlifting Club), and British Weightlifting – I feel lucky to be involved in weightlifting in a country where the sport is well run and accessible to all with a level playing field. Special thanks go to Sam Dovey, who taught me to lift and has mentored me throughout my coaching career, always urging me to 'be the best you can be'. Finally, I would like to thank my co-author Mihai Ivan, who gave me my first taste of success as a coach and has taught me more than I did him.

My final words are for you, the reader. It is our firm hope that this book can start some future champions on the path to greatness. International competition may seem like a long way away now but remember, all of the greatest lifters started where you are now and built their success one kilogram at a time. If you believe in yourself, you will be surprised at what you can achieve.

PART 1

GET STARTED

CHAPTER 1

INTRODUCTION

C ongratulations! With this book, you are taking your first steps into one of the world's most exciting sports.

Olympic weightlifting has grown in popularity in the last few years and looks set to continue to do so. Not only is it a fantastic sport in its own right but athletes from other sports are turning to the Olympic weightlifting movements as the best way to develop explosive power.

Even if you do not go on to compete in Olympic weightlifting at a high level, learning and practising the movements brings all kinds of benefits. As well as the obvious strength and power gains, weightlifting can teach you a lot about your own body and mind. Lifting heavy things overhead also builds confidence in your own abilities like almost nothing else.

Weightlifting can have a reputation for being difficult. It is true that getting really good can take a lifetime and the challenge of lifting more always remains. However, anyone can learn the basics in a short time and in this book we will show you how.

WHO IS THIS BOOK FOR?

This book is mainly aimed at people who are new to the sport of weightlifting but it will also be useful for anyone who is still learning the lifts. We assume no experience at all of barbell training but we also give specific guidance for those who have already trained, for example in powerlifting.

The book will also be valuable for athletes from other sports who want to use the weightlifting movements in their training (and if you are an athlete in virtually any sport, you should be using them!)

Lastly, anyone who does CrossFit® will find it useful to set a good foundation by learning the right way to snatch and clean and jerk.

WHAT WILL THIS BOOK DO FOR YOU?

We will take you to the stage where you can successfully complete the main weightlifting movements (snatch and clean and jerk) along with the most important assistance exercises (squats, presses, deadlifts and pulls). At that point, you will be ready to follow a beginners' training programme such as the one we present at the end of the book.

HOW TO USE THIS BOOK

Weightlifting is not something you can learn and get better at just by reading. We recommend that you get into a gym and start practising right from the start, whether with a coach or on your own.

The book is structured in the order which we think it makes sense to approach things, starting with testing and, if necessary, improving your mobility in part one. In part two, you will learn the Olympic weightlifting movements. Parts Three and Four look at the various assistance exercises that you will use in your training for strength and power. We finish the book in Part Five by discussing how weightlifters train, nutrition and your future as a lifter.

The appendices at the end of the book include a glossary of weightlifting words that you may not be familiar with, sources of more information and some example training programmes that you can use to get started.

In chapter 2, we talk about the value of coaching. Assuming you find a good coach, listen to them and try to follow what they tell you to do, despite anything we tell you in this book. They will have their own way of doing things, which may be slightly different to ours, particularly when it comes to programming. This is fine - there are different approaches to learning the movements that have got results in the past for different people.

If you don't have a coach, read the advice in chapters 2 and 15 on how to make the best of self-coaching and use the programmes in appendix three to give you a structure to work to. The first of these is specifically designed to guide you through the mobility tests and drills from part one and the techniques in part two.

WHAT IS WEIGHTLIFTING?

If you're reading this book, you probably know that there is a difference between the sport of weightlifting (all one word) and lifting weights (two words). Just in case, let's be clear about what this book covers. There are several sports and activities that involve lifting weights:

Weightlifting is an Olympic sport that involves lifting a barbell over-head in two different ways: the snatch, where it goes overhead in a single movement, and the clean and jerk, where two separate movements are used. Olympic weightlifting is what this book is about.

Powerlifting is a strength sport that uses three movements – the squat, the bench press and the deadlift.

Strongman is a strength sport that uses a wide variety of events, often including movements based on weightlifting and powerlifting.

Bodybuilding means training to achieve an aesthetically pleasing physique. It can be done competitively or just to look good. Bodybuilding training will often involve lifting weights but has very different priorities from the sport of weightlifting.

A BRIEF HISTORY OF WEIGHTLIFTING

Lifting heavy things competitively has a history going all the way back to ancient times, but weightlifting as we recognise it today dates back to the 19th century. Strength contests using both barbells and dumbbells are recorded in Britain and continental Europe at that time. Mostly these were ad-hoc, local affairs but in 1891, E. Lawrence Levy of England was crowned as the first world weightlifting champion.

In the early days, most competitions consisted of performing lifts for repetitions, so had more in common with modern strongman events than the sport of weightlifting as we know it now.

In 1896, weightlifting made its first appearance at the modern Olympic games, for men only. Two events were contested – two- and one-handed versions of what we now call the clean and jerk.

Weightlifting appeared at the Olympics off and on until 1920, when it became a permanent fixture and weight categories were introduced.

In 1924, the two-handed press and snatch were added. Four years later, in 1928, the one-handed lift was removed, leaving a three-lift event that lasted until 1972. At that point, the clean and press was removed (it was deemed impossible to accurately judge when lifters were leaning back too far), leaving us with an event very much like weightlifting today.

Towards the end of the 20th century, women started getting involved in weightlifting, with the first women's world champions named in 1987. However, it wasn't until 2000 that women were included in the Olympics.

Since 1972, the most significant rules changes have been adjustments to the weight categories in 1992 and 1997, which also meant that there were new world records to be set. In 2017, a new women's 90+ weight category was added and in 2018 the weight categories will be changed again to meet requirements from the International Olympic Committee.

THE COMPETITION LIFTS

As we mentioned earlier, currently two lifts are used in weightlifting competitions – the snatch and the clean and jerk.

In the snatch, the bar is lifted from the platform to above the head in a single movement.

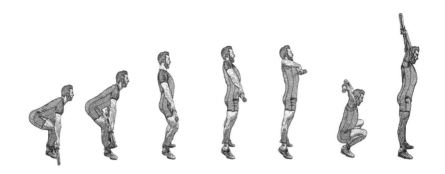

The Snatch

In the clean and jerk, the bar is first lifted to the shoulders (the clean) and is then lifted above the head (the jerk).

The Clean and Jerk

We will look at the clean in detail in chapter 8 and the jerk in chapter 9.

CHAPTER 2

WHAT YOU NEED

I n this chapter, we will look at what you will need in order to make progress in weightlifting, along with the equipment that is required to do weightlifting training. We will also discuss the importance of coaching and what to do if you can't find a coach.

THE FIVE ESSENTIALS FOR SUCCESS

Contrary to what you might think, weightlifting is not all about raw strength. Of course, being strong certainly helps and is a requirement to lift big weights. However, you will also need to lift the weight efficiently if you want to fulfil your potential.

Lifting efficiently brings with it a couple of important requirements. You need the **mobility** to get into good positions (particularly the ability to squat deep to catch the bar as low as possible in the snatch and the clean). You will also need good **technique** to move the bar well, make best use of your body's leverages and maintain your balance.

Only once you have good mobility and technique should you start focusing on developing the **strength** to lift heavier weights. Along with strength, you will also need to train the related but separate quality of **power** – the ability to deliver force to the bar quickly. The competition lifts feature some of the fastest movements in sport so you will need to use your muscles quickly.

The final essential you will need is the **discipline** to stick to a training programme. Getting good at weightlifting requires a lot of time to develop mobility and technique, along with heavy strength training that will leave you tired and aching. There is no easy road – every new personal best has to be fought for. Weightlifting is not an easy sport by any means, but that is part of why we love it.

So, the five essentials of weightlifting are:

- Mobility – to get into the required positions
- Technique – to lift efficiently
- Strength – to lift heavier weights
- Power – to move the bar fast when required
- Discipline – to stick to a training programme.

Don't worry if you don't feel strong in these areas already – they can all be improved and doing so is part of what makes weightlifting an immensely satisfying and beneficial sport.

After this chapter we will look at each of these five essentials in detail.

As well as these five personal attributes, you will also need somewhere to train and the right equipment to train with. It is also really beneficial to get some coaching. We'll spend the rest of this chapter looking at these things.

EQUIPMENT

Weightlifting does require some equipment but it is not the most expensive of sports. The most costly things you need will last virtually forever if they are looked after, and can be shared by many people. Joining a weightlifting club or a good gym will give you access to most of the required equipment so you may just need to invest in a pair of weightlifting shoes and a gym membership.

Bar

The bar is the fundamental piece of equipment in weightlifting. Each bar consists of a few parts:

Rotating Sleeve   Knurling   Rotating Sleeve

The Barbell

The rotating sleeves enable the part of the bar that we hold to spin freely, which is important for the Olympic weightlifting movements.

The knurling is the pattern of ridges on the bar that help with grip. The pattern of the knurling can vary from bar to bar, so when you are using an unfamiliar bar it is a good idea to check your grip widths as described in chapters 7 and 8. Knurling can also vary in its sharpness – sharper knurling will make it easier to grip the bar but can be painful or even cause skin tears on the hands. We look at how to look after your hands in chapter 15.

In competition, two different bars are used – one for men, one for women. Both take the same kind of plates (with 50mm holes) but there are some differences. The men's bar weighs 20kg compared to 15kg for the women's bar and is slightly longer and thicker.

	Weight	Grip Diameter	Length
Men's Bar	20kg	28mm	2200mm
Women's Bar	15kg	25mm	2010mm

Not long ago, it was unusual for many gyms to have women's bars even if they had everything else required for weightlifting. Happily this is changing and any good weightlifting gym will have both kinds of bar.

You may also come across lighter bars, known as technique bars. These come in a range of weights, usually around 5-10kg. They are great when you are getting started – as the name implies, they enable you to focus on technique before you start using the full-weight bars. As soon as you can lift a proper bar with 5kg plates on, you should use one of those.

Whatever kind of bar you use, it is important to make sure that it is designed for Olympic weightlifting. Olympic weightlifting bars differ from powerlifting and general strength training bars, which may look very similar. Olympic bars are designed to flex when lifted with significant weight on them but this is not important for a beginner. More crucial is the way that Olympic bars are designed with rotating sleeves to hold the plates. This means that during a lift, the central part of the bar can freely rotate, which enables you to maintain your grip on the bar while moving around it. If you use a bar without rotating sleeves, you will run into problems at some point.

Bars come in a range of prices. At the top end of the market are brands like Eleiko, Uesaka and Werksan. They make the bars that are used in international competition but also have some slightly cheaper training bars. For more affordable options, brands like Rogue, ESP, American Barbell , Vulcan and York offer decent quality bars.

Higher-end bars typically use needle bearings for the best possible rotation of the sleeves. Cheaper bars tend to use bushings, which do not rotate quite so smoothly but are fine for most people.

The general rule is that you get what you pay for, with high-end bars being more robust and having better sleeve rotation. Paying more will usually get you a longer warranty period. However, as a beginner, you don't need to use a top of the range international competition standard bar. Get the best bar you can afford but as long as your bar comes from a reputable company and is designed for Olympic weightlifting, it will be okay to learn with.

If you decide to buy second-hand, watch out for bars that have not been looked after. Even a good bar can end up not rotating properly or even bent if treated badly. This is especially a problem when bars are used for other things than Olympic lifting. Trying to do Olympic weightlifting movements with a damaged bar will be more difficult and potentially dangerous.

You should also beware of damaged bars in gyms, especially where they are used by people who are not weightlifters and may have mistreated them. Good weightlifting gyms will have separate bars for things like squats to avoid this.

Looking after a bar is easy if you follow some simple rules:

- Don't drop the bar unless it has bumper plates on it (see the next section)
- If you use a bar in a rack, unload it immediately after you finish your training
- If you use metal racks, put something in the hooks (e.g. straps – see later in this chapter) to avoid damage to the knurling on the bar
- Service the rotating sleeves according to the manufacturer's instructions.

If you look after it, a high-quality bar will last you a lifetime.

Plates

The key consideration for the plates that we use to add weight onto the bar is protection of the bar, the plates and the surface we are lifting on when we drop the bar after a lift. For this reason, we use bumper plates, which are coated in rubber and are designed to survive being dropped.

Bumper plates come in a variety of sizes. Full-size plates are all 450mm in diameter but come in different thicknesses – competition plates are fairly thin, while less dense, thicker bumpers are often used in gyms that don't have designated lifting platforms as they are kinder to concrete floors.

Smaller plates at lighter weights are known as 'change' or 'fractional' plates. These are generally used alongside full-size bumper plates.

Plates designed for weightlifting will usually be in kilograms but you may come across plates in pounds. They will be either black or coloured according to this table:

Colour	Metric	Imperial
Red	25kg, 2.5kg	55lbs
Blue	20kg, 2kg	45lbs, 5lbs
Yellow	15kg, 1.5kg	35lbs
Green	10kg, 1kg	25lbs, 2.5lbs
White	5kg, 0.5kg	10lbs, 1.25lbs

As with bars, bumper plates come at a range of prices with more expensive plates tending to last longer.

Watch out for rubber-coated plates that are not actually bumper plates – these cheaper plates are not designed to be dropped and will start to fall apart after some use. Like bars, decent quality bumper plates will last a very long time so it's worth getting proper ones.

You may also come across technique plates that are made of hollow plastic and are much wider than normal plates. These are usually 2.5kg or 5kg. These are great to use when you are getting started but are not required – you can always use blocks or even a stack of plates to raise the empty bar to the right height to practise as if it had plates on it.

Collars

We use collars to keep the plates tight on the sleeves of the bar and prevent them sliding around. With some bar and plate combinations, collars are not always needed, but if in doubt, use them. Collars come in a few different types:

 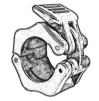 

Collars

- Spring collars – the kind found in most gyms
- Plastic clip collars – these are a bit easier to take on and off quickly but they do tend to get broken so expect to replace them reasonably often
- Competition collars – these are designed to hold the plates very securely with a lock and screw mechanism. Unlike the other types of collar, these have significant weight (2.5kg each) which should be added to the weight of the bar and collars.

Platform

It is important to lift on a stable surface that will not be damaged by drop-ping the bar and plates onto it. The ideal is a dedicated platform with a hard surface under your feet – usually this is some kind of wood. Plywood works but can peel off in layers over time. A plywood base with an MDF surface is more durable. Often the wooden strip will be flanked by rubber areas for the bumper plates to land on, reducing wear and tear on the wooden portion. Many gyms are now using hard rubber floors that are suit-able for weightlifting.

In competition, the platform will measure 4m x 4m, but for training purposes you only really need around 3m x 2m of space.

Shoes

The one piece of personal equipment that you absolutely should invest in is a pair of weightlifting shoes. These have a couple of features that help with the Olympic lifting movements:

- Raised heels make it a bit easier to get into deep squats

- Hard soles will not compress with heavy weights like normal trainers will.

A Weightlifting Shoe

There is now a selection of weightlifting shoes available at a range of price points, from around $60/£50/€50 to around $200/£150/€150. Adidas, Nike and Reebok all have offerings, along with a range of smaller brands. The important thing is to find a pair that has a good solid raised heel and fits you snugly – you don't want any movement of your feet inside the shoes when lifting.

Clothes

In competition, there are strict rules about what weightlifters must wear, including having to wear a tight singlet. For training, you can wear whatever you are comfortable in, providing that it will enable you full movement and will not get in the way of the bar. T-shirts and shorts are fine as long as they are not too baggy.

Long socks can be a good idea, to provide some protection for your shins from bars with sharp knurling. You can get socks marketed specifically for weightlifting but any long sports sock will do.

Chalk

Lots of lifters use magnesium carbonate, usually called 'chalk' to prevent sweat on hands from affecting the grip. Most of the time it is not really required as long as the knurling on the bar is reasonable. However, many weightlifters use chalking their hands as part of their pre-lift ritual, so they do it every time.

Most gyms that have the equipment for Olympic lifting will provide chalk or be happy to let you bring your own but there are some that don't allow it due to the mess that it can make. An alternative in this case is 'liquid chalk' that comes in a bottle and has a solvent that evaporates after you apply it to your hands. This kind of chalk stays on the hands much longer and does not make so much mess. Be warned though, it takes a fair bit of scrubbing to get it off the hands at the end of your training session!

Belt

A belt can provide support for the lower back and make it easier to brace the core during lifts. Belts are typically worn for heavy clean and jerk and some assistance exercises such as squats. You don't really need one until you start lifting some serious weight. In fact, it is good to avoid using a belt until you need to – if you rely on a belt too early, you will miss out on some important core strength development.

Straps

Straps are used to relieve the weight on the hands, avoiding overworking the grip. They can also help to reduce wear and tear on your hands. Like belts, it is a good idea to use them only when required. You want to develop you grip strength but, when you start lifting bigger weights, you may find that your hands start to suffer from overuse. When that happens, you can start using straps for heavier sets of snatches, pulls, deadlifts and some other exercises.

Finger/Thumb Tape

Many weightlifters use tape on their fingers and thumbs to protect them from damage. You probably won't need to do this when you are getting started but if you find the hook grip painful (see chapter 4), you should try using some tape on your thumbs.

Knee Sleeves and Wraps

Traditionally, weightlifters have used long strips of material wrapped around the knees to provide some extra support. Many still do this but there is now also the option of using a purpose-made neoprene knee sleeve.

As well as providing some support for the knee, knee sleeves will warm the knee up more quickly and keep it warm during a training session.

While they can be helpful, knee sleeves or wraps will not make you stronger and, if they are too thick, can limit mobility enough to make lifts harder.

Blocks

Blocks are used for two main purposes in weightlifting training. The snatch and the clean can be performed from varying heights of block to focus on a specific part of the movement. Higher blocks can also be used when just doing jerks so that the bar is dropped back on the blocks rather than to the floor between each rep.

Blocks can also be very useful when you are getting started with snatches and cleans and you don't want to put any extra weight on the bar. If you use blocks at the right height, you can start lifts with the empty bar at the same height as it would be with plates on it. If you don't have access to blocks, you can stack spare plates up to get the same effect.

Racks and Power Cages

When doing squats and some other assistance exercises, you will need to take the bar out of a rack for each set and return it afterwards. You can also use a rack to train jerks on their own if you don't have access to jerk blocks. Racks come in a variety of shapes and sizes, from separate stands for each end of the bar to full cages with adjustable safety bars. Which kind you use doesn't matter too much, as long as the rack is sturdy and can be adjusted to a height that you are comfortable with.

Squat racks and power cage

Foam Roller

In chapter 5 we will look at how foam rolling your muscles can help to improve your mobility.

A foam roller

To get the best results, you want to use a fairly dense roller. Often these are black but manufacturers make them in a range of colours.

Rollers come with a wide variety of textures. There is no best option here so, if possible, try a few out and choose what works best for you.

COACHING

Weightlifting is a sport where success is very dependent on having good technique. For that reason, it is crucial that you learn good technique as quickly as possible and correct any technical flaws as soon as you can. Using an inefficient technique for any length of time will make it harder to learn a better way to do it.

The best way to learn good technique and correct problems is under the guidance of an experienced coach. They will lead you through a progression to learn the lifts and provide feedback on your lifting during training sessions. As you get more experienced, a coach will give you training programmes appropriate to your needs to ensure you are doing the right amount of training. If you decide to compete, your coach should support you in preparing for competition and, if they are sufficiently local, on the day itself.

It is important to work with a coach who has the right level of experience. To this end, most national governing bodies for weightlifting have certification or licensing systems that can provide a level of confidence that a coach knows their stuff. See Appendix Two for some contact details. However, don't rely on certificates alone – when considering a coach, find out how much actual coaching experience they have, what success their athletes have had and, if possible, speak to some people that they have already coached.

Many weightlifters move into coaching as they approach the end of their own competition careers. While it can be great to learn from someone who has made big lifts themselves, a strong competition record is not a guarantee that a lifter will have the knowledge, communication skills and patience required to be a good coach.

Another important factor when deciding which coach to work with is personality. Every coach has their own style and what works for one lifter will not work for another. If you want to progress as a weightlifter, you will have to work hard during training sessions but you will also want to enjoy them – your relationship with your coach will be a big part of that.

The best way to get access to good coaching is to join a reputable weightlifting club. A club will typically have one or more coaches who lead training sessions where multiple lifters train together. This environment is great for progressing – training alongside more experienced lifters enables beginners to learn a lot more quickly than on their own. This kind of training will also be a lot more affordable than being coached one on one.

Online Coaching

Many coaches are now willing to coach lifters remotely by looking at videos of lifts and using phone calls, online chats or messages to provide feedback. While not as good as getting direct feedback during a training session, this is certainly better than no coaching at all and worth considering if you do not have a good coach close by.

The earlier advice for finding a good coach applies to online coaches – check their credentials and experience and, if possible, talk to some people who have used their services already. One thing to do is to make sure you are clear on what you will be getting for your money – how often can you expect to get input from the coach.

Self Coaching

If you find it impossible to find a coach or just can't afford one, your only option may be to coach yourself. This is by no means ideal but some people are able to make it work.

If you go down this route, you will need to diligently record and review every set that you do during each training session, critically analysing each lift to check whether there is anything that you need to adjust. Don't wait until after the session – watch each set as you rest after it so that you can make changes straightaway.

One option is to join an online forum where you can share videos for feedback from other lifters. This can be useful but watch out for 'armchair experts' who sometimes critique such videos without any real experience or rely on textbook answers that don't apply universally.

Probably the most important thing you can do if you can't find a good coach is to find some good training partners. Training with other weightlifters, especially if they are a bit better than you, can provide great motivation and more pairs of eyes to spot technical issues.

PART 2
MOBILITY

"Nothing is softer or more flexible than water, yet nothing can resist it."

LAO TZU

CHAPTER 3

MOBILITY REQUIREMENTS

I n order to be able to use the most efficient techniques for weightlifting, you will need to get your body into some specific positions. The most obvious examples of this are the deep squats used in both the snatch and the clean; the deeper you can squat to catch the bar, the less height you need to put on the bar earlier in the lift. If your mobility is limited then this will restrict what you can do and will mean you will have to use less efficient movements.

Some lucky beginners have excellent mobility already – this is particularly true of younger learners or those with a background in a sport with high mobility requirements, such as gymnastics. If you fit into this category then you just need to make sure you maintain your level of mobility while getting stronger.

Others have more challenges. If you are coming to the sport at an older age then you will likely have at least some mobility issues that you need to work on, whether from muscle tightness caused by activity such as running or postural issues due to desk work and driving.

Your proportions can also make specific aspects of mobility harder. Long legs can make squatting deep more difficult while certain arm proportions can make the front rack position uncomfortable.

Don't worry though: even if you have mobility restrictions, you will still be able to learn the Olympic weightlifting movements in some form. Throughout this book, we will note when you can adapt the movements to take account of your level of mobility.

In an ideal world, you would have perfect mobility before learning the technical aspects of the lifts. However, for most people it is more realistic to begin learning while working on mobility in parallel. As your mobility improves, you will be able to get into progressively better positions.

SQUATTING

In both the snatch and the clean, as well as in squat assistance exercises, it is important to be able to get into a deep squat while keeping the torso as upright as possible and not rounding the back.

Back rounding is something you should watch out for – this is when your back bends forwards. Lifting significant weight with a rounded back will put your spine at risk, so should be avoided.

A deep squat in a good position is only going to be possible if you have good mobility in your thoracic spine, hips, knees and ankles.

Back squat, front squat and overhead squat

If you are tight around your thoracic spine, you won't be able to maintain the flat back position and avoid rounding, especially if you try to force yourself into a deeper position than you are actually capable of.

How well you can flex your hips will go a long way to determining how deeply you can squat. You will also need to be able to fully bend your knees (not a problem for most people unless you have an injury) and have good dorsiflexion at the ankle (the ability for the shin to come forwards over the foot).

The overhead squat position used in the snatch adds the additional requirement to be able to keep the bar overhead, which challenges the mobility of your shoulders. This can especially be a problem for anyone who has done lots of training in exercise that leads to tight pectorals (press ups, bench press) or lats (pull ups)

If you want to use a squat jerk style, the shoulder mobility requirement is even tougher to meet as you will almost certainly be using a narrower grip width on the bar. Along with a much smaller margin of error, this is one of the reasons why most people do not use this style of jerk.

Squat jerk catch position

The front squat and the clean have a different upper body mobility requirement. The 'rack' position used to hold the bar on the shoulders in front of the lifter can be difficult for many people to start with due to tightness in the shoulders, arms and wrists.

Rack position

For the split jerk, you need to be able to keep the bar over the shoulders and get the head forward, often described as 'getting your head through', while splitting your legs forward and backward.

Split position in a jerk

CHAPTER 4

TESTING YOUR MOBILITY

Y ou can get an idea of which aspects of mobility you need to work on by working through the following set of simple tests. Each one challenges the mobility in a different part of your body.

SCAPULA WALL SLIDE

Stand with your back against a wall. Make sure your ankles, bottom, shoulders and head are all in contact with the wall. Hold your arms against the wall in the position shown in the first picture below. Now slowly move your arms into the second position, trying to keep everything in contact with the wall.

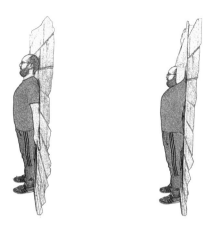

Scapula wall slide

If you can't perform this movement while keeping everything touching the wall, you may well have some mobility issues in your thoracic spine.

HIP FLEXION TEST

Lie on a bench or table (a bed can work if it is reasonably hard) with your lower legs hanging off so the edge is behind the knees. One at a time, pull each of your knees towards you while keeping your other leg in contact with the surface you are on. If you can't get your knee all the way to your chest without the other leg moving away from the surface, you have a hip flexion limitation that you should address.

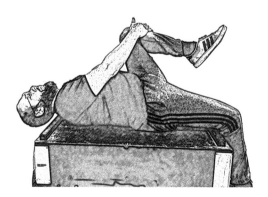

Thomas hip flexion test

ANKLE DORSIFLEXION TEST

Stand close to a wall, facing it. One side at a time, place a foot around 10cm from the wall and try to touch the wall with your knee while keeping your foot flat. If you can manage it, increase the distance and try again. The longer the distance you can achieve, the better your dorsiflexion. If you can't manage the original 10cm, this is definitely an area you should work on.

Ankle dorsiflexion test

SHOULDER RESTRICTION TEST

Lie on your back on the floor. Stretch your arms out over your head and touch the floor with your thumbs. Now bring your knees to your chest and try to do the same again. If you can't, it is likely that you have tight lats.

Shoulder restriction test

PUTTING IT TOGETHER

So far, we have been testing mobility at individual joints or areas of the body. Now we'll try some movements that use multiple joints.

Air Squat

Stand with your feet around shoulder-width apart with toes pointing slightly outwards. With your arms out in front of you, squat down while trying to keep your torso upright and your arms parallel to the floor, level with your shoulders.

Air squat

You may find that you need to adjust your feet slightly to find the position that enables you to get into the deepest possible squat. This is normal – everyone's hips are unique so different stance widths and foot angles work for different people.

If you can manage a deep air squat with arms in front of you, try with your hands behind your head.

Snatch Grip Press

Now grab a broomstick and put it on your shoulders, holding it with a nice wide grip. Push the stick up, straightening your arms. You should be able to keep the stick over your shoulders.

Snatch grip press

We will look at how to find the perfect grip for the snatch in chapter 7. For now, just use a width you are comfortable with.

Overhead Squat

Hold the stick overhead in the same position you used for the last exercise. Stand in the same stance that you used for air squats and squat as deeply as you can, staying as upright as you can in your torso. Keep the broomstick over your shoulders and your shoulders over your feet. You will find that you need to rotate your shoulders to keep the stick in the right place. It will be useful to get someone else to watch you or record yourself from the side to check that the stick is not moving forwards in front of your feet.

Overhead press

Don't be surprised if you find it hard to achieve a deep overhead squat. This movement (which includes the bottom receive position of the snatch) is something that many people find challenging when they do it for the first time.

Front Squat

For our final mobility test, you will probably need to use a weightlifting bar rather than a broomstick. This is because most people need a reasonable amount of weight to push against to hold their hands and arms in a proper rack position.

Lift the bar onto the front of your shoulders, balancing it in place using your hands, keeping your elbows as high as possible. You may find this an uncomfortable position – if so, this is something you will need to work on.

Front squat rack position

Now, position your feet like you did earlier and squat down, keeping your torso upright with your elbows high and the weight of the bar on your shoulders. Go as low as you can without your back rounding or your elbows dropping. Ideally, you want to be able to get all the way to your deepest possible squat.

Front squat

CHAPTER 5

IMPROVING YOUR MOBILITY

D on't worry if the tests in the previous section showed that you have some mobility challenges that need to be addressed. In this section, we will look at a whole range of exercises you can use to rectify these problems and achieve much better mobility.

THE KEY

Whatever your mobility challenge, the most important thing is to try to work on it every day. Fifteen minutes a day of mobility work is much more effective than an epic session once per week.

Decide what areas you need to work on and commit to doing something to improve them every day, even if only for a few minutes. Progress will seem slow at first but with every session you will become more mobile and in a surprisingly short time you will be moving much better.

TYPES OF MOBILITY WORK

There are several distinct types of work you can do to improve your mobility:

- Static Stretching – this is what most people associate with mobility. Stretching the muscles can help to make them less tight, enabling better mobility.
- Dynamic mobility exercises – these involve more movement, progressively improving mobility
- Foam Rolling – using a roller (or sometimes a ball) to massage muscles, loosening tight spots
- Sports Massage – a more intense massage than foam rolling, performed by a professional.

Stretching

The main consideration for stretching is to avoid stretching muscles that have not been warmed up. Stretching cold muscles reduces the effectiveness of the exercise and can even do more harm than good. For this reason, stretching is usually done at the end of training sessions. However, it can be useful to do some stretching before training to be able to get into better positions – just make sure to do some dynamic warm-ups first.

If you want to do stretching outside of training sessions (if you have mobility issues then you should!), make sure to warm up first or stretch after a hot bath or sauna.

Dynamic Mobility Exercises

Movements that assist with mobility make great elements of a warm-up before weightlifting training. In chapter 17 we look at some of these.

Foam Rolling

Applying pressure to muscles to reduce tightness is properly called 'self-myofascial release' but pretty much everyone refers to it as 'foam rolling' due to the most common tool that is used.

The idea is to apply pressure to areas of the fascia (the soft connective tissue that surrounds muscles), to reduce tightness, enabling easier movement of the muscles.

There is some evidence that foam rolling can help with increased range of motion and can reduce soreness from training.

The basic technique of foam rolling is to put the roller on the floor and use your own body weight to apply pressure. Move the roller up and down each muscle until you find a tender spot. Then, maintain pressure on that spot for around thirty seconds to a minute. This will be painful to some extent but should not be unbearable.

There is a huge range of foam rollers available. Most manufacturers offer a range of hardness levels, usually identified through the colour. You will get better results from harder rollers, albeit with a bit more discomfort. There are even battery-powered vibrating foam rollers on the market now. There is some limited evidence that these might give faster results but don't expect these expensive tools to change your mobility overnight!

As well as actual foam rollers, you can use a whole range of other implements to achieve the same goal. Hard balls, such as those used in lacrosse or field hockey are popular.

Sports Massage

A professional sports massage has the same goals as foam rolling, usually with a more intense approach.

One thing to note is that usually you will want at least twenty-four hours' recovery after a proper massage before training.

UPPER BODY MOBILITY

If you are having problems maintaining overhead positions, your problem could be with mobility in your shoulder girdle or it could be something else that is affecting the positions you can reach. Your thoracic spine could be the culprit or tight muscles such as the pectorals could be to blame. Tight pectorals are often an issue for anyone who has done lots of bench presses, so if you are coming from a powerlifting or bodybuilding background, you may need to do a lot of work to loosen them up. A lot of the time, the root of the problem isn't in the upper body at all but to do with poor hip mobility, although better upper body mobility can help to offset this, so it's still worth working on.

If you work through all of the exercises here and those in the following sections, you should address the vast majority of potential issues.

To stretch out the muscles on your front, find a corner or doorway and put one arm on the edge, vertically. Now turn away, feeling the stretch on the front of your shoulder.

Corner stretch

Repeat this stretch a few times on each side.

If you have a helper available, another great stretch for the front of your upper body is to kneel with your hands behind your head and have someone pull your elbows gradually backwards until you feel the stretch.

Partner stretch

Now, grab a broomstick and hold it in one hand with your elbow high. Reach around behind your back with the other hand, grab the stick and pull downwards. You should feel the stretch under your shoulder.

Stick stretch

While you have the broomstick, put your elbows on a block at about waist height. Hold the stick so that your hands are wider apart than your elbows. Now, bend over and push your head down between your arms. You should feel the stretch on your upper arms.

Upper arm stretch

The last exercises that you can use the stick for are called shoulder dislocations. Don't worry – they don't actually involve dislocating your shoulders!
Hold the stick at your waist with a wide grip and straight arms. Now,
keeping your arms straight, rotate them up and over your head. Keep
rotating your arms until either tightness stops you going any further or you
have rotated all the way until the stick is touching your back. If you made
it all the way, move to a slightly narrower grip and go again.

Shoulder dislocations

Ideally, you want to use a grip width where you can just make it all the
way over, feeling a bit of a stretch as you go. If you can't do this even with a
really wide grip, just go as far as you can and hold the stretch for a few
seconds each time.

Shoulder dislocations work well as part of a warm-up before training – do a few sets of ten reps.

For the final shoulder exercise, you will need a squat rack or power cage that is good and stable – ideally attached to the floor.

Put the bar in the rack and hold it in your hands. Now move your feet away from it so you are leaning at about a forty-five degree angle. Drop your head between your arms and feel the stretch across your back.

Upper back stretch

If you don't have a suitable rack or cage for this, you can use a wide, heavy block at about waist height and put your hands on the edge of it to achieve a similar stretch.

Foam rolling the upper back can help a lot with upper body mobility – it's a good idea to do this before every training session if you have any problems in this area.

Foam rolling the upper back

An often-neglected part of the body when it comes to mobility is the wrists. Wrist mobility can be important for getting into a good rack position during the clean and jerk.

You can stretch your wrists by kneeling and placing your hands flat on the floor in front of you, then gently moving your weight forward over them.

Wrist stretch one

Then, turn your hands around to point towards you and repeat the same process.

Wrist stretch two

Finally, turn your hands so that their backs are on the floor and stretch again.

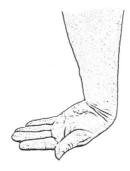

Wrist stretch three

Be careful not to put too much weight on your wrists in this position.

Hip Mobility

If you struggle to get into deep squats, the cause is often tightness around the hips, especially in the hip flexors (the muscles that connect the top of your legs to your hips).

To stretch your hip flexors, start off on one knee, with your foot out in front of you. Put your hands on your hips, stay upright and push your back foot downwards, as if you are trying to push it through the floor.

Hip flexor stretch

You should feel the stretch around your hips. If you don't, try moving your front foot further forward.

If the basic version of the hip flexor stretch is too easy for you, try elevating your back foot on progressively higher blocks or benches.

Elevated hip flexor stretch

You can even use a wall for the ultimate stretch.

Another good way to stretch the muscles around the hip is with a very long lunge position.

Long lunge stretch

You can stretch some slightly different muscles around the hips by getting into a deep squat position and pushing your knees outwards using your elbows.

Squat stretch

LEG MOBILITY

The big muscles of the legs are ideal candidates for foam rolling – both during warm-ups and when you are working specifically on mobility.

The traditional quadriceps stretch, pulling one leg at a time up and backwards can be useful.

Quadriceps stretch

Hamstrings can be stretched either standing or on the floor.

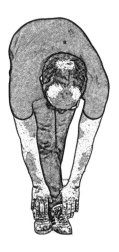

Hamstring stretch

The best way to stretch the calves is to stand on the edge of a step with the weight on the front of each foot in turn and lower your ankle.

Calf stretch

ANKLE MOBILITY

The most popular way to stretch your ankles to improve dorsiflexion is to get into a squat position and use a weight to push the knees down, either both together with a barbell or separately using a weight plate.

Weighted ankle stretch

Start with a very light weight and work up gradually. You can moderate the intensity of the stretch by moving your own bodyweight forwards or backwards.

GENERAL MOBILITY

As well as the previously described exercises that address specific parts of the body, it is a good idea to do some exercises that challenge the mobility of your whole body in positions that will be important in the Olympic lifts.

Use a broomstick to do overhead squats, holding yourself in the deepest position you can with your weight on your heels and the stick above your feet.

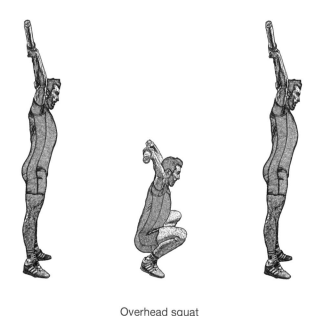

Overhead squat

Get a kettlebell, dumbbell or something else conveniently heavy, hold it in front of you just under your chin and do goblet squats, again holding the deepest position in which you can stay upright.

Goblet squat

Goblet squats are also great as a warm-up before other kinds of squats or Olympic lifting. We will look at goblet squats some more in chapter 8.

PART 3

TECHNIQUE

"Get out of your own way. Let your training take over."

MATTIE ROGERS

CHAPTER 6

TECHNIQUE FOUNDATIONS

I n the next three chapters, you will be learning the movements that make up the snatch and clean and jerk lifts. Before we look at them, there are some basic things that, if you get them right from the start, will make a big difference as you progress.

PROPRIOCEPTION

To get good at weightlifting, you need to understand your own body and what it is doing. This sense of where the different parts of you are and how they are moving is called proprioception.

Like any other skill, proprioception is something that you can improve by practising it. The most important way to do this is to constantly be consciously thinking about what you are feeling and doing as you perform exercises.

One thing to avoid is training in front of a mirror. While it may seem useful to watch yourself and perhaps correct movements, using a mirror for this can actually make you less aware of what your body is doing, reducing your proprioception. It is much better to record yourself doing an exercise, watch the video and then make adjustments. Fortunately, these days almost everyone has a good video camera with them all of the time in the form of a smartphone.

Over the coming chapters, we will be introducing you to lots of positions and movements. As each new thing is presented, take the time to think about it and, more importantly, feel it as you practise. It can even be useful to close your eyes briefly while holding a position, to really focus on feeling how your limbs and joints are related, how your weight is distributed and so on.

WEIGHT BALANCE

A specific aspect of proprioception that is important in weightlifting is to be aware of how your weight is distributed between your feet and between the front and back of your feet.

You should always keep your weight (and that of the bar you are lifting) evenly distributed between your feet, even in the split jerk where each foot will have a different kind of contact with the platform.

As we discuss the lifts, the required weight balance on the foot will vary for different parts of the movements. The important thing is to be aware of whether your weight is on the front of your feet, mid-foot or on your heels, and whether you need to make an adjustment.

BREATHING

The movements in weightlifting are completed so quickly that oxygen intake is not a factor, at least during individual reps. However, it is still crucial to take control of how you are breathing.

The most important effect of breathing is in maintaining tightness in the core. After taking a big breath in and holding it, it is much easier to lock the core tight by pushing out against the abdominal muscles. After breathing out, the core is weaker and it is much more likely that tightness will be lost, which can lead to rounding the back, which we want to avoid both for safety and as an important part of proper technique.

Most of the time, you want to take a big breath in before executing a movement and hold that breath in until the movement is completed.

You can further tighten your core by performing what is known as the Valsava technique. To do this, keep your airway closed but try to exhale against it. You should notice that your diaphragm moves downwards and you feel the abdominal pressure increasing.

EXPLOSIVENESS

Some parts of the weightlifting movements need to be completed as quickly as possible, with the maximal amount of energy being imparted to the bar in a very short time. We call the ability to do this explosiveness.

A classic example of a simple movement that requires explosiveness is a vertical jump. If you slowly bend your legs and straighten them, you will not even leave the floor. Perform the movement more quickly and you will jump. To reach the maximal height, you will need to contract your muscles as quickly as possible, delivering as large a force as possible over a very short time.

ARM TENSION

For much of the weightlifting movements, we actively avoid using our arms to lift the weight, fighting the years of experience that give us the instinct to use our arms to lift things. We do this because we need our arms to bend to keep the bar close to us and to be able to move fast at the right times. Arms that are tight cannot move fast.

We can't keep our arms loose through the whole of the lifts though. We have to use our arms to pull ourselves under the bar at the right time. Once the bar is overhead in the snatch and the jerk, we have to rapidly lock our arms out and keep them locked. So an important skill is to be able to control the tightness of our arms.

Try this exercise to feel the difference between tight and loose arms. Stand with your arms by your side. First, tense your arms and jump upwards. Notice how your arms either stay by your side or swing out in front of you. Next, loosen your arms (it can help to give them a bit of a shake) and jump again. Don't do anything actively with your arms. You should notice that your hands now move up close to you as your loose elbows bend.

BACK TIGHTNESS

When we are lifting heavy weights, it is vital that we keep our spine in a position where it is strong and protected from harm, even when in a deep squat. The ideal is a flat back that is locked tight to prevent it from flexing.

Flat back

You want to avoid rounding of the back and also having too exaggerated an arch.

For most people, achieving a flat, tight back under load involves retracting the shoulders to counteract the tendency of the bar to pull the upper back forwards.

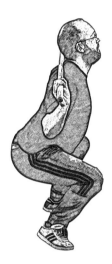

Rounded back and over-arched back

A good way to think about retracting the shoulders is to get someone to place the side of their hand on your back between your shoulder blades. Now, try to squeeze their hand by pushing your shoulders back.

If you do this while weightlifting before you start each lift and keep back tightness through the whole lift, it will protect your spine and enable you to maintain the positions that you need to be in for efficient lifting.

HOOK GRIP

Using the correct grip on the bar is crucial to success with heavier weights, so you might as well get used to it as soon as possible. In the hook grip, the first two or three fingers are positioned over the thumb, trapping it between them and the bar:

Hook grip

The big benefit of the hook grip is that it means you don't have to use such a tight grip to hold the bar. This means that your arms can be kept more relaxed which, as we will see, is really important.

To be completely honest, the hook grip can be uncomfortable, even painful for while. This does pass as you get used to it and the huge advantage is worth it. To start with, you can use hook grip for part of your training sessions and switch to a non-hooked grip if it becomes painful. Taping the thumb can help to some extent but really you just have to get used to it.

CHAPTER 7

THE SNATCH

The snatch rightfully has a reputation as one of the most explosive movements in all of sport. The bar is lifted from the platform and locked out above the head of the athlete in a single movement that takes less than a second.

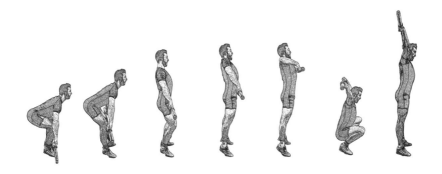

The snatch

Mastering the snatch is challenging but, when it goes right, it looks and feels amazing to put something heavy overhead with such apparent ease.

In competition, the snatch is the first lift performed and can set the tone for the contest. Compared to the clean and jerk, it tends to favour fast, technically brilliant athletes.

The snatch is a complex exercise with lots of moving parts so we usually talk about it in terms of a few different phases:

- The **first pull** where the bar is lifted from the floor to the knees
- The **transition** from first pull to second pull, which takes the bar up to the top of the thighs
- The **second pull**, where maximum power is used to drive the bar upwards in front of the body
- The **drop** in which the lifter pulls themselves down into a deep squat and catches the bar overhead
- The **recovery** where the lifter stands up with the bar overhead.

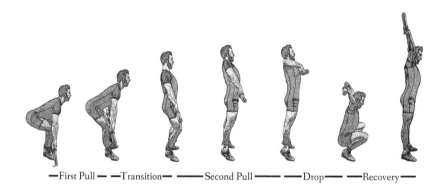

—First Pull— —Transition— ——Second Pull—— ——Drop— —Recovery—

Phases of the snatch

While each of these phases demands different things to get right, a good snatch puts them all together to produce a single, seamless movement.

LEARNING THE SNATCH

In order to become proficient in the snatch, you will need to move the barbell in an efficient way. The speed of the movement and the challenge of the overhead squat position mean that even small imperfections can cause a miss. For this reason, it is vital that you learn the correct movement right from the start.

Trying to attempt a complete snatch right away is not the best way to learn it. Rather, it is best to divide it into parts and incrementally add more to the movement. This can be done by starting from the beginning of the lift but we recommend working in reverse. Starting with the catch and recovery means that you can see how each movement that you add contributes to those that follow it.

Many coaches use the bottom-up approach and, if you have a coach who prefers that approach, you should follow that. Both approaches work very well but we find the reverse chain approach is easier for people who don't have constant coaching input.

Follow these steps in order to work towards completing a full snatch. Don't rush through them – give yourself plenty of time with each step to get it right. Record yourself completing each step and review the video between sets.

We will go through the following steps:

1. Find your grip width.
2. Overhead squat.
3. Snatch balance.
4. Scarecrow snatch.
5. Hip snatch.
6. Hang snatch from above the knee.
7. Hang snatch from shins.
8. Full movement.

You'll be working with just the bar for the whole of this progression – adding weight can come later.

Let's get started!

STEP 1 – FIND YOUR GRIP WIDTH

Before you can start to learn the snatch, you will need to decide how wide your grip should be. While some lifters have different preferences, for most of us, the best grip width puts the bar in the hip crease when standing with straight arms, so this is the best starting point.

Finding your grip width - bar at hips

A good method for testing your grip width is to stand holding the bar with your arms relaxed. Now raise one leg – you should be able to bring your leg up so the top of your thigh is horizontal without moving the bar. If the bar moves, it is too low and you probably have a grip width that is too narrow. If the bar is not in contact with your legs at all, your grip with is probably too wide.

Finding your grip width - raising a knee

Once you have found the right grip width, take a look at where your hands are relative to the ring markings in the knurling on the bar. You can use these to get your hands in the same place every time without repeating the process above.

Measuring your grip width

Watch out for bars that have non-standard markings - if in doubt when using a different bar, test your grip width to make sure it is right.

STEP 2 – OVERHEAD SQUAT

Grab the bar using your snatch grip and put it on your shoulders. Press the bar overhead and lock your arms at full extension. Squat down as deep as you can while keeping the bar over your shoulders and your shoulders over your feet. This is important – if the bar is forward or backward of your feet, a heavier weight will mean that it will pull you off-balance, likely causing you to miss a lift.

Overhead squat

Pause for a second or two at your deepest position. This is where you want to receive the snatch so you need to be comfortable and balanced here.

STEP 3 – SNATCH BALANCE

We use the snatch balance to practise the fast drop under the bar that we need in order to perform a good snatch. Before doing the movement fast, it's a good idea to try it slowly. Put the bar on your shoulders again, holding it with your snatch grip. Put your feet at the same width you used for the overhead squat. Now squat down as you did for the overhead squat and press the bar simultaneously. The feeling you are aiming for is that you are moving yourself around the bar rather than moving the bar upwards.

Slow snatch balance

Once you are happy with the slow version of the snatch balance, try the fast version. Put the bar on your shoulders again but have your feet a bit closer together than for the overhead squat – about hip-width apart is good. This time, rather than squatting and pressing the bar, drop as quickly as you can into your snatch receive position and simultaneously punch out your arms to full lockout. During the drop, you will also need to move your feet outward to your overhead squat width.

Fast snatch balance

You may find that it helps to initiate the fast drop under the bar if you rise up onto your toes just before dropping. This has the added benefit of replicating the position you will be in just before you drop under the bar in the full snatch movement.

You may see some lifters 'heaving' the bar upwards at the start of a snatch balance movement. This is only required when performing the movement with significant weight on the bar. For the purpose we are using it here – as a step towards learning the snatch – we don't want to do that. Focus on dropping quickly under the bar and catching it at your full overhead squat depth.

STEP 4 – SCARECROW SNATCH

Now we will practise how we will get under the bar as it rises up in front of our body in the snatch.

Hold the bar with your snatch grip with your feet hip-width apart and pull the elbows upward and backward to position the bar across your chest. Move onto your toes and then rapidly pull yourself under the bar to your snatch receive position.

The important thing here is to think in terms of pulling yourself under the bar with your arms rather than pulling the bar upwards.

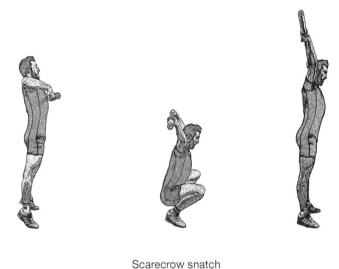

Scarecrow snatch

STEP 5 – HIP SNATCH

Now we're ready to introduce the idea of driving the bar upwards before we pull ourselves under it.

Hold the bar with your snatch grip at waist height. Bend the knees slightly and ensure your torso is vertical. Your shoulders will be just slightly behind the bar. Many people call this the 'power position' as it is from this position that we apply our maximum power to the bar.

Now, explosively extend your hips and knees to propel the bar upward. If you keep your arms relaxed, they should naturally bend as they allow the bar to move. When the bar reaches the position we used for the scarecrow snatch, pull yourself under it just as you did before.

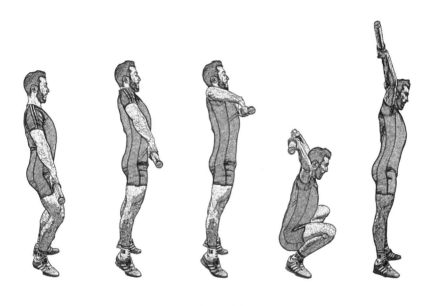

Hip snatch

It is important that you don't bump the bar forwards off your hips. If you focus on vertical drive, you should find that your hips meet the bar rather than driving through it.

STEP 6 - HANG SNATCH FROM ABOVE THE KNEE

We will now move the bar lower down the legs to incorporate the transition phase of the snatch.

Start from the power position again but this time rotate forwards at your hips to move the bar down your thighs until it is just above the knees. At this position, your shins should be around vertical and your shoulders should be over the bar.

Now, smoothly reverse the movement you just made to return the bar to the hips. Practise this a few times before moving on. If you are self-coaching, this is a really good time to film yourself a few times and check that both positions are correct.

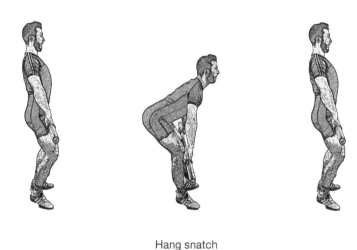

Hang snatch

When the movement from knees to hips feels good, perform a hip snatch at the end of the movement.

STEP 7 – HANG SNATCH FROM SHINS

You are almost ready to put some plates on the bar and do a snatch from the platform. We just need to establish your start position. A good way to do this is by continuing the process of doing hang snatches from progressively lower positions.

Repeat the hang snatch movement from the previous stage but this time, when the bar reaches the knees, bend your knees to lower the bar further, to mid-shin. During this movement, your back angle should remain fixed. Reverse the movement, bringing your shins back to vertical to return the bar to the knees. You should be using your legs only for this part of the movement. Practise this a few times.

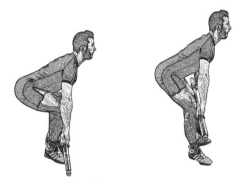

First pull from shins to knees

This is the part of the snatch called the first pull. This can be a slightly misleading term because you don't really want to be consciously pulling at all. It is better to think in terms of pushing the platform with your feet. If you keep your back tight and your arms loose, the bar will be towed off the platform without you having to think about pulling it.

When you are happy with the movement from mid-shin to the knees, proceed as you did for the previous step, performing a hang snatch.

Hang snatch

STEP 8 – FULL MOVEMENT

All that remains now is to put some light plates on the bar (or raise the bar on blocks) and perform a full snatch. If you have been using just the bar so far, it is a good idea to put some technique plates on and try some hang snatches first, to get used to a bit of extra weight.

When you are ready to attempt a full snatch, get yourself into a good start position, as we discussed earlier. Then carry out the full set of movements that you have practised – use your leg to move the bar to the knee, then your hips to bring the bar up the thighs to the power position. Explosively extend hips and knees before pulling yourself under the bar to your receive position.

If all goes well, you will have completed a full snatch.

REFINING YOUR SNATCH

Unless you are an incredibly lucky natural, your early attempts at the snatch will leave a lot to be desired. This is normal. You now need to improve your technique, making it as efficient as possibly before you start attempting big weights.

The biggest mistake that new lifters make when learning the snatch is to put too much weight on the bar too early. Trying to learn the positions and movements with too high a weight is counter-productive. The extra weight causes you to revert to instinct and lift using a bad movement pattern. It is much better to practise with light weights until you are happy with how you are moving. You should then spend some time drilling this movement pattern to make it feel natural.

When correcting issues, it is best to start with the beginning of the lift – the start position – and work forwards from there. Any error early in the lift will affect the rest of the movement, so you need to make sure that each position and phase is right before moving on to later ones.

We will now take a close look at the key positions and movement phases in the snatch. Record yourself and pause the video at each of these positions to check whether you have them right.

Start Position

Getting the perfect start position can take a bit of playing around. The main variables are the width of your feet and the position of the bar over them.

Start with your feet about hip-width apart, toes pointed slightly outward and the bar over the first joint of your toes (usually this will be about where your laces end). Now bend your knees and hips enough to be able to get your hands to the right grip width on the bar. Get your back nice and tight and adjust your position so that your shoulders are over the bar. Your arms should be fully extended and loose so that they hang vertically.

Snatch - start position

You should feel the weight right under where the bar is – at the first joint of your toes.

Consistency in the start position is really important. If you change your position even slightly between each lift, the results will be magnified as the lift progresses.

First pull

This phase of the movement gets the bar off the platform and to the knees. As we mentioned earlier, the name of this phase can be misleading. You want to feel that you are using your legs to push the platform with your feet, not pulling with your arms and back.

For beginners, the most important thing to focus on in the first pull is to get into a good position when the bar reaches the knees. If you rush the movement, this will be more difficult, so push smoothly with your legs.

It is important that the bar moves vertically or slightly back towards you off the platform – if it moves forwards, the weight will pull you off-balance and prevent you getting into good positions later in the lift.

During the first pull, the weight on your feet should move backwards, staying under where the bar is. By the time the bar reaches the height of the knees, it should be around mid-foot, just in front of your ankles.

Bar at Knees

There are two ways that the bar can get past the knees. Either the knees get out of the way of the bar or the bar moves forward to move around the knees. Since any unnecessary horizontal movement of the bar is something that we want to avoid, by the time the bar reaches the knees, they clearly need to have moved out of the way. This means that in this position, the shins will be close to vertical.

Snatch - bat at knees

By now, the weight balance on our feet should be further back than it was at the start – just in front of the ankles.

Aside from the bar lifting to the height of the knees and the knees moving back out of the way, we want to maintain the rest of our position from the start of the lift. This means that our back angle will match the start position. A common error in this position is for the hips to be too high compared to the shoulders, leading to a much more horizontal back than we want and the shoulders being way out in front of the bar.

Transition

In this phase, we bring the bar from the knees up to the top of the thighs, ready for the big second pull.

This part of the movement uses the hips rather than the legs. In fact, the knees will actually bend slightly rather than continuing to extend. This 'double knee bend' movement means that when we do fully extend in the second pull, we have a bigger angle at the knee to play with to drive the bar upwards.

Like the first pull, for beginners the most important thing in this phase is to get into a good position for the next part of the lift, so to start with stick to a speed that enables you to move the bar consistently to the right place.

During the transition, your shoulders will move backwards relative to the bar so that you will end up with them behind the bar. Your weight should remain mid-foot throughout – don't come so far back onto your heels that your toes come up off the platform.

Bar at Top of Thighs

The position of the bar just below the hips is often called the 'power position' because it is the position from which we want to deliver the maximum power into the bar.

Snatch power position

You should have your knees slightly bent, your torso upright and your shoulders slightly behind the bar. At this point, the weight balance on the feet should be at mid-foot, ready for the powerful vertical propulsion of the second pull.

Second Pull

This is the phase that does the most to drive the bar upwards quickly to the height it needs to get to for the catch.

In the second pull, you will extend forcefully at your knees and hips, bringing your hips forward to meet the bar. Don't extend so far that you bump the bar away forward though – that will lead to it looping out in front of you and being much harder to receive in the catch. Think in terms of the hips coming 'to the bar, not through the bar'.

During the second pull, it is especially important to keep your arms loose – if they are tight, the bar will only be able to go forwards as it comes up.

Full Extension

To put maximum vertical drive into the bar, you will need to reach a position where you are extended up as tall as you can get.

Snatch extension

Note that your arms should still be long and loose at this point – it is only after the full extension that you engage your arms to pull under the bar.

Drop

This is another phase that is slightly confusingly named. Here we don't just drop and let gravity do the work; we actively pull ourselves under the bar, bringing our elbows up and back to keep the bar close to us.

The key thing to keep in mind here is that we are moving ourselves around the bar rather than trying to pull the bar higher.

During this phase, most lifters will jump their feet out to a slightly wider position for the receive. Try to do this with the minimum of elevation of the feet from the platform. Jumping the feet too far off the platform is sometimes called 'donkey kicking'. We want to avoid it as it does not contribute to the lift and can make us slower to get into the receive position.

Receive Position

The lower you can catch the snatch, the less the height you will need to propel the bar during the second pull. Therefore, the receive position is all about being in as deep an overhead squat as possible while maintaining your balance.

Snatch receive

Use whatever foot width and angle will enable you to get into the deepest overhead squat that you can perform while keeping the bar over the back of your head, shoulders and feet. If the bar is forward of this position in the receive, you will lose heavier lifts as the weight of the bar pulls you forward.

Recovery

Standing up from the receive position basically involves doing the concentric (upwards) part of an overhead squat.

The important thing here is not to rush to stand up. Make sure you have your balance before driving with your legs through your heels to get to the finish position.

Finish Position

In competition, weightlifters have to finish in a position where they are standing with their feet level with each other and in line with the bar. Although you are not competing yet, you might as well get into the habit of finishing in the correct position.

Snatch finish

COMMON PROBLEMS WITH THE SNATCH

The snatch is a complex movement that takes everyone some time to get right. Here some of the most common mistakes to look out for:

Not Staying over the Bar

In order to move the bar vertically, your shoulders need to be right above the bar from the start of the lift to when you apply maximum force to it. At this point, they will move back relative to the bar but until then, stay over!

Pulling with the Arms

Your arms should be long and loose until you have driven the bar upwards and you are ready to pull yourself down into the catch position. If you pull with your arms, they will be tight. This will lead to the bar looping out in front of you.

Pulling Early

If you start your explosive second pull too early, the bar will move away from you and end up too far forward.

Driving Hips through the Bar

If you drive your hips forwards too much, they will drive right through the bar, bumping it forwards and away from you. Some contact between bar and hips is expected but if you are hitting the bar hard, try to focus more on upwards propulsion.

Lack of Acceleration

You should be accelerating during the snatch movement. Aim for a controlled pull from the floor that turns into a very explosive second pull.

Not Fully Extending

At the end of the second pull, you should be fully extended vertically, with your whole body in a straight line. If you record yourself and you never reach this position before dropping under the bar, you need to focus more on this.

Feet too Wide in the Catch

When you catch a snatch, your feet should be at the same width you would use for an overhead squat. It is common for beginners to spread their feet too wide rather than getting into a deep squat. This is sometimes known as 'starfishing'.

Weak Lockout

When you punch out your arms overhead to catch the bar, make sure you keep pushing the lockout. If you are at all casual with it, you will struggle with heavier weights. Often, lifters will assume that they need to strength work to get better at locking out. While this is true to some extent in the long run, often the immediate problem is not making enough effort to keep the arms completely locked.

TRAINING THE SNATCH

For beginners, snatches are usually best trained in sets of two or three reps with a relatively light weight. The important thing is to use a weight that enables you to deliver the best technique that you can. You can add weight gradually as your confidence increases.

Once you progress beyond very light weights, you will need to do some warm-up sets before your top-weight work sets. Keep jumps between sets small – adding more than 5kg to the bar for snatches can lead to problems for beginners as the change is significant. It's better to do some extra warm-up sets than to rush to the work sets and mess them up.

Your aim as a beginner should be to make as many good reps as possible. If you miss reps or have reps that don't feel good, lower the weight.

There are some variations of the snatch that may appear on a programme or that a coach may ask you to use:

Hang Snatches

Rather than starting with the bar on the platform, lift it to waist height before bending your knees slightly to get into the power position. Then bend at the hips to lower the bar into position (see step 6 of the progression earlier in this chapter) and start the lift.

When you use hang snatches as an assistance exercise (rather than just as a learning tool as we did earlier), you want to use the stretch reflex from your muscles. Don't pause at your start position – just lower the bar, feel the bounce from the stretch reflex and start the movement.

Make sure to maintain your back tightness all the way through the hang snatch movement – a common error is to lose tightness as you lower the bar into position.

You can do hang snatches at a variety of heights. The higher the position, the more the focus is on dropping under the bar quickly, as you won't be able to drive the bar so high. Really high hang snatches are called hip snatches. Other common positions are mid-thigh, and just below the knees.

Something to watch out for on hang snatches is your arms getting tight. This can happen because of the extra time spent holding the bar. Focus on keeping the arms long and loose until the second pull is complete. Using straps (see chapter 2) can be useful for learning to keep the arms loose as they remove the grip challenge.

Many lifters hold onto the bar throughout a set of hang snatches but it can be a good idea to drop it to the platform and reset between reps. Doing this helps to keep your arms loose and also means you can ensure your feet are in the right position and your back is locked for every rep.

Block Snatches

Block snatches work in a very similar way to hang snatches but they avoid the problem of tight arms from holding onto the bar for longer.

Like hang snatches, block snatches can be done from a variety of heights depending on what the goal is.

Working from the block is a great opportunity to perfect a particular position in the snatch movement or to train a part of the movement where you are weak. If you are self coaching, before starting to do reps, it's a good idea to record yourself in position with the bar on the blocks to check you have it just right.

Paused/Halting Snatches

This variation works just like a normal snatch but you pause briefly in key positions, usually at the knee and mid-thigh.

This is useful for ensuring you are reaching these key positions and also for focusing on how they feel.

As with the hang snatch, watch out for arm tightness caused by the extra time holding the bar.

CHAPTER 8

THE CLEAN

The clean is the first part of the Clean and Jerk. In the clean, we move the bar from the platform to shoulder height so we can catch the bar much lower in the clean than in the overhead position required for the snatch. Because the bar does not have to move as high, we typically use larger weights for the clean compared to the snatch.

The clean

In competition, the clean (as part of the clean and jerk) is performed after the snatch. It tends to favour athletes with more raw strength and, because larger weights tend to be used, will often decide the result.

The good news is that, once you have learned the basics of the snatch, you should find learning the clean much easier. It is a simpler movement and you will find that many of the same cues and concepts are useful.

Like the snatch, the clean is usually divided into several phases:

- The **first pull**, where the bar is lifted from the floor to the knees
- The **transition** from first pull to second pull, taking the bar to mid-thigh
- The **second pull**, where maximum power is used to drive the bar upwards
- The **drop**, in which the lifter pulls themselves down into a deep squat and catches the bar
- The **recovery**, where the lifter stands up with the bar on their shoulders.

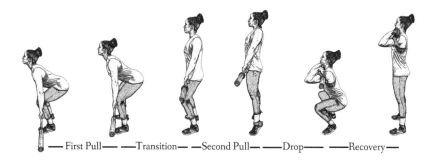

— First Pull— —Transition— —Second Pull— —Drop— —Recovery—

Clean phases

While each of these phases requires different things to be done at the right time, in a successful clean they all come together in a single movement.

LEARNING THE CLEAN

Although the clean is a little less complex than the snatch, it still makes sense to learn it in stages rather than just trying to do the whole thing right away. As with the snatch, we recommend learning it in reverse, starting with how you will catch and recover and working down to lifting from the platform. If you have a coach, they may take the opposite approach, starting from the platform. That is absolutely fine and many lifters have learned successfully with both approaches.

We will use the following steps to work towards the full clean:

1. Find your grip width.
2. Rack position.
3. Front squat.
4. Hang clean pull.
5. Hang power clean.
6. Hang clean from mid-thigh.
7. Hang clean from knee
8. Hang clean from mid-shin
9. Full Clean

STEP 1 – FIND YOUR GRIP WIDTH

In the clean, you will use a much narrower grip than you did for the snatch. Essentially, you want to have your hands as close together as possible without your arms getting caught on your legs as you complete the movement. This puts your arm close to vertical when you lift the weight from the floor.

Finding your clean grip width

As with the snatch, you should use hook grip to hold the bar during the clean. You will most likely release your hook grip as you catch the bar, in order to get into your best possible rack position.

One you have found your grip width, check where your hands are relative to the markings in the bar knurling.

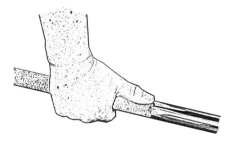

Measuring your grip width

STEP 2 – FIND YOUR RACK POSITION

The biggest difference between the snatch and clean is that you will now be catching the bar on the front of your shoulders rather than overhead. We looked at the mobility requirements for this position in chapter 1. To be able to clean substantial weights, it is vital that you develop a strong rack position.

In a good rack, the weight of the bar rests on the shoulders, not on your hands. If you take the weight on your hands, you will find it much harder to keep your arms loose. It is essential to have relaxed arms if you are going to quickly punch them out in the jerk that will follow the clean in a competition lift.

Rack position

Most people cannot get into their best rack position while maintaining a hook grip, so you will most likely release your hooks as you catch the clean. In fact, many lifters do not even maintain a full grip on the bar in the rack position, just using their fingers under the bar to balance it on the shoulders. This is fine – as long as the bar is secure in the rack position, you do not need a tight grip on it.

The best exercise for testing your clean rack position is the front squat (see chapter 8). Before you start learning the clean, it is a good idea to spend some time doing front squats with enough weight on the bar to get into a good rack position. This will help you to build the confidence to catch the bar in a good, deep clean.

STEP 3 – FRONT SQUAT

Start by putting the bar into a good rack position and performing the deepest front squat that you can, without rounding your back or dropping your elbows. Hold the position at the bottom for a few seconds each time. This will be your clean catch position.

You will notice that in the clean catch position, the bar is a lot lower than it was in a snatch.

Front squat

STEP 4 – HANG CLEAN PULL

Now stand with feet hip-width apart, gripping the bar so your hands are just outside your legs. Bend your knees slightly, get your back tight and rotate at your hips to bring the bar down to around two thirds of the way up your thighs. Keep your arms long and loose. Then extend your hips and knees to propel the bar upwards. If you keep your arms loose and your knuckles down towards the ground, the bar will come up close to your body.

The main thing here is that you want the bar to move vertically, not forwards. A common mistake is to hit the bar too hard with the thighs, bouncing it out in front and making the clean much harder.

Hang clean pull

STEP 5 – HANG POWER CLEAN FROM MID-THIGH

Next, you will do exactly the same thing but when you have extended, whip your elbows through under the bar and drop into a shallow squat to catch the bar in your rack position.

Hang power clean

STEP 6 – HANG CLEAN FROM MID-THIGH

You will almost certainly find that the first time you catch a hang clean with the bar, you will catch it in a high power clean position. Moderate the power of your pull so that you only drive the bar upwards to just above the height of your clean catch position. Now you will have to drop down fast to catch the bar. This is one of the keys to a good clean.

Hang clean

STEP 7 – HANG CLEAN FROM KNEE

Position yourself as before with the bar at mid-thigh. This time, rotate at your hips and push them back to move the bar down your thighs to your knees. You should feel some tightness in the back of your legs. You should also find that your knees naturally come back so that your shins are vertical. Once you reach the knees, reverse the movement and perform a hang clean as before.

Hang clean from knee

STEP 8 – HANG CLEAN FROM MID-SHINS

As before, bring the bar down to knee height. Now bend at your knees to lower the bar to mid-shin height. If you are using plates, go down until they touch the floor. If not, just approximate the height of a pair of plates and go down that far. During the descent, try to keep your back angle the same as it was when the bar was at the knees.

The position you reach now is likely to be a good starting point for where you will want to start from when cleaning from the platform, so take a moment or two to feel and remember it.

Clean start position

You now just need to reverse the movements, using your legs to bring the bar to knee height and then your hips to bring it two thirds of the way up your thighs before extending to drive the bar upwards and dropping to catch it.

STEP 9 - FULL CLEAN

Now, you just need to put some light plates on the bar (or raise the bar to an equivalent height using blocks), get yourself into the start position you found in the previous step and perform a clean.

Use your legs to bring the bar to the knees, then your hips to bring it to mid thigh before driving upwards and dropping under to catch in your rack position. Finally, stand up and celebrate your first full clean!

REFINING YOUR CLEAN

As with the snatch, it makes sense to spend some time improving your technique with lighter weights before aiming for maximal lifts. Compared to the snatch, most lifters can put a bit more weight on the bar with the clean and it can actually be useful to do this.

We will now take a close look at the key positions and phases of the clean. Record yourself and pause the video at each of these positions to check whether you have them right.

Start Position

Position yourself with your feet around hip-width apart, with the bar over the balls of your feet. Grip the bar with your arms just outside your legs and keep your arms long and loose. Make sure your back is tight and flat. Bend your knees so that your shoulders are over the bar.

Clean start position

Because of the position of the bar, your weight will be on the first joint of your toes.

First Pull

As with the snatch, focus on getting into a good position when the bar reaches the knees. If you rush the movement, this will be more difficult, so push smoothly with your legs.

It is important that the bar moves vertically or slightly back towards you off the platform – if it moves forwards, the weight will pull you off-balance and prevent you getting into good positions later in the lift.

During the first pull, the weight on your feet should move backwards, staying under where the bar is. By the time the bar reaches the height of the knees, it should be around mid-foot, just in front of your ankles.

Bar at Knees

When the bar reaches the knee, your shins should be close to vertical. This will mean your knees are out of the way, allowing the bar to continue moving vertically as it rises. Your back should be at the same angle as it was in the start position and your arms should still be long and loose.

By now, the weight balance on your feet should have shifted back towards the heels.

Aside from the bar lifting to the height of the knees and the knees moving back out of the way, we want to maintain the rest of our position from the start of the lift. This means that our back angle will match the start position. A common error in this position is for the hips to be too high compared to the shoulders, leading to a much more horizontal back than we want and the shoulders being way out in front of the bar.

Clean - bar an knees

Transition

In this phase, we bring the bar from the knees up to mid thigh, ready for the big second pull.

This part of the movement uses the hips rather than the legs. In fact, the knees will actually bend slightly rather than continuing to extend. This 'double knee bend' movement means that when we do fully extend in the second pull, we have a bigger angle at the knee to play with to drive the bar upwards.

Like the first pull, for beginners the most important thing in this phase is to get into a good position for the next part of the lift. To start with, stick to a speed that enables you to move the bar consistently to the right place.

During the transition, your shoulders will move backwards relative to the bar so that you will end up with them behind the bar. Your weight should remain mid-foot throughout – don't come so far back onto your heels that your toes come up off the platform.

Bar at Mid-thigh

One difference between the snatch and the clean is that in the clean, the key contact point is mid-thigh rather than at the hip crease. When you reach this position, you should have a slight knee bend, your back angle should be more vertical and your arms should still be straight and loose, ready for the second pull.

Clean - bar at mid-thigh

You should have your knees bent, your torso upright and your shoulders slightly behind the bar. At this point, the weight balance on the feet should be at mid-foot, ready for the powerful vertical propulsion of the second pull.

Second Pull

This is the phase that does the most to drive the bar upwards quickly to the height it needs to get to for the catch.

In the second pull, you will extend forcefully at your knees and hips. Don't extend so far that you bump the bar away forward off your thighs though – that will lead to it looping out in front of you and being much harder to receive in the catch.

During the second pull, it is especially important to keep your arms loose – if they are tight, the bar will only be able to go forwards as it comes up.

Extension

The extension in the clean will not bring the bar as high as in the snatch – assuming you have good mobility, it is possible to get very low in the catch position, so you only need to pull the bar a little bit higher than that. If you pull the bar higher, you will either catch high and perform a power clean or you will drop into a full clean and the bar will 'crash' onto you, making you unstable in the catch position. It is, therefore, good to learn the height you need to pull the bar to for a clean and try to do that consistently.

Clean extension

Drop

In the drop phase of the clean, we need to pull ourselves down to the deep position where we want to catch the bar and also get our elbows through into the rack position.

Timing is everything in this part of the lift. If we drop too far under the bar, it can crash onto us, making it very hard to catch. It is much better to maintain contact with the bar as we drop so that we get into a good rack position just as we want to lock tight in the catch.

Catch

The main thing you want to avoid when catching the clean is letting the bar slip forwards off your shoulders. To do this, you need to be sitting as upright as you can with elbows high and a tight back. Your weight will be on your heels

Clean catch position

Final Position

After standing up from a clean, you will often be preparing for a jerk. You should have your feet around hip-width apart and be holding the bar in a good rack position, with elbows as high as is comfortable.

Clean finish

COMMON PROBLEMS WITH THE CLEAN

Watch out for these common errors as you are practicing the clean:

Not Staying over the Bar

In order to move the bar vertically, your shoulders need to be right above the bar from the start of the lift to when you apply maximum force to it. At this point, they will move back relative to the bar but until then, stay over!

Pulling with the Arms

Your arms should be long and loose until you have driven the bar upwards. If you pull with your arms, they will be tight. This will make you slower to get your elbows through under the bar.

Pulling Early

If you start your explosive second pull too early, the bar will move away from you and end up too far forward.

Lack of Acceleration

You should be accelerating during the clean movement. Aim for a controlled pull from the floor that turns into a very explosive second pull.

Pulling too High

It is common for beginners to imagine that the bar needs to get a lot higher in a clean than it actually does. This either leads to doing a power clean (see chapter 12), being too slow to drop under the bar or dropping under deep and the bar crashing down onto the shoulders.

You should be dropping and catching the bar as soon as you have applied maximum force to it. Continuing to pull after that will only make the lift harder.

Not Meeting the Bar

If you focus too much on dropping deep as quickly as possible, you will find that you become separated from the bar, which will then crash down onto your shoulders.

You should aim to maintain contact with the bar, racking it as soon as you are able to. This may mean with lighter weights you catch the bar a bit higher. That's better than the bar crashing down onto you and ruining your catch.

Slow Arms

A common way for beginners to miss cleans is with their elbows too low, meaning the bar rolls forward out of the rack position. You need to be as fast as possible to get your elbows through under the bar and establish a strong rack.

Caving in the Catch

If you don't lock everything tight when you catch the bar, the weight will either pull you forward, rounding your back (due to a lack of back tightness) or push you in too deep (due to a lack of leg tightness).

TRAINING THE CLEAN

For absolute beginners, cleans are usually trained on their own in sets of two or three reps. Once the jerk has been learned and you are confident with the clean, you should start to train clean and jerk together, usually with sets of two reps.

There are some common variations of the clean that you may come across on a programme or a coach may instruct you to use.

Hang Cleans

Rather than starting with the bar on the platform, stand up straight with the bar and bend the knees slightly to get into the power position. Then, lower the bar into position (see earlier in this chapter), feel the stretch reflex and start the movement.

You can do hang cleans at a variety of heights. The higher the position, the more the focus is on dropping under the bar quickly, as you won't be able to drive the bar so high.

Something to watch out for on hang cleans is your arms getting tight. This can happen because of the extra time spent holding the bar. Focus on keeping the arms long and loose until the second pull is complete.

Many lifters hold on to the bar throughout a set of hang cleans but it can be a good idea to drop it to the platform and reset between reps. Doing this helps to keep your arms loose and also means you can ensure your feet are in the right position and your back is locked for every rep.

Block Cleans

Block cleans work in a very similar way to hang cleans but they avoid the problem of tight arms from holding onto the bar for longer.

Like hang cleans, block cleans can be done from a variety of heights depending on what the goal is.

Working from the block is a great opportunity to perfect a particular position in the clean movement or to train a part of the movement where you are weak. If you are self-coaching, before starting to do reps, it's a good idea to record yourself in the start position to check you have it just right.

Paused/Halting Cleans

This variation works just like a normal clean but you pause briefly in a key position such as at the knee.

This is useful for ensuring you are reaching these key positions and also for focusing on how these positions feel.

As with the hang clean, watch out for arm tightness caused by the extra time holding the bar.

CHAPTER 9

THE JERK

The jerk is how we get the bar from our shoulders to above our heads in the clean and jerk. Usually when we use the term 'jerk' with nothing else to qualify it, we are talking about the split jerk. This is by far the most common way to get the bar from the shoulders to above the head in the combined clean and jerk movement.

The split jerk

As the name implies, in a split jerk the lifter drops into a split position, with one leg forward and one back, to catch the bar overhead.

While the jerk can seem simpler than the snatch and the clean from a technical point of view, it is uniquely challenging in that you will have the weight on you before you start it. The psychological effect of feeling the weight can mean that a willingness to commit to completing the lift can be just as important as technique and power in order to get a big jerk.

Other kinds of jerk include the power jerk (see chapter 12), where a shallow squat is used in the catch, and the squat jerk where a deep, narrow-grip overhead squat is used. We will look at the squat jerk at the end of this chapter.

The split jerk is the most popular variation for competition use for a few reasons. It provides better depth under the bar than a power jerk, meaning that the bar doesn't need to be driven so high in order to catch it. While it's possible to catch deeper in a squat jerk, the tough mobility and leg strength requirements of the squat jerk (see later in this chapter) mean that most lifters can do better with a split jerk.

The biggest benefit of the split jerk over the other variations is that the forward/back split of the legs gives more margin for error when driving the bar upward. Unlike in the power and squat jerks, if the bar is not quite driven fully vertically, it is possible to rescue a split jerk by shifting onto the front or back foot. Of course, we want to drive as vertically as possible but the ability to adjust saves many lifts that would otherwise be lost.

We usually talk about the split jerk in four phases:

- The **dip**, where the lifter bends their legs
- The **drive**, in which the bar is pushed explosively upwards
- The **split** ,where the legs move forward and backward into the split position
- The **recovery** to standing straight

———Dip——— ———Drive——— ——— Split ——— ———Recovery——

Split jerk phases

LEARNING THE SPLIT JERK

We will use the following steps to learn the split jerk:

1. Choose your front foot.
2. Split position.
3. Splits without the bar.
4. Overhead press in split position.
5. Dip, drive and catch in split position.
6. Recovery.
7. Standing dip drive and catch.
8. Split jerk

STEP 1 – CHOOSE YOUR FRONT FOOT

Let's start by establishing which foot should go forward when you split. Stand on a platform with plenty of space in front of you. Get someone to stand behind you and, without warning, push you gently but sharply forward. You will instinctively move one of your feet to keep your balance. This foot will usually be the better one for you to use to split jerk.

Push test to choose front foot for split jerk

Whichever foot you choose, once you start practising the jerk, stick to the same front foot. The split movement needs to become instinctive – alternating between front feet will just make this harder.

STEP 2 – SPLIT POSITION

Next, you need to establish a strong split position. You want a position that satisfies these points:

- Front foot is flat on the floor
- Front knee is not ahead of front foot – the shin should be around vertical
- Back knee is bent so that the thigh is around vertical
- Back foot is on ball of foot
- Feet are about shoulder–width apart
- Weight is balanced between front and back feet.

Stand with your hands on your hips and experiment with your split position until you find something that feels stable and meets the points above.

Split position

It will be useful to mark your best split position on the platform with tape – you can then ensure you are reaching this position in the later steps.

STEP 3 – SPLITS WITHOUT THE BAR

When you have a position you are happy with, practise moving quickly from the start position of the jerk (hip-width apart) to the split, with your hands on your hips.

Splits without the bar

Your feet should not come a long way off the floor during the movement. Focus on trying to land your feet in the same places every time.

What you are looking for here is for your torso to remain vertical and drop downwards without moving forwards or backwards.

STEP 4 – OVERHEAD PRESS IN SPLIT POSITION

The next step is to get into your split position with a weightlifting bar in front rack position. Do some overhead presses in this position.

You will need to move your head back to allow the bar to come up vertically in front of it. As soon as the bar has passed, push your head forward again so that the bar is over your shoulders.

Hold for a second or two at the top of each press, making sure your arms are fully locked and you feel stable and balanced.

Overhead press in split

STEP 5 – DIP, DRIVE AND CATCH IN SPLIT POSITION

Now, instead of pressing the bar, dip very slightly in your split and pop the bar up off your shoulders, catching it at arm's length. Your feet should not leave the floor. This is simulating how you will catch the bar at the end of the jerk. Do a few sets like this to get used to catching the bar.

STEP 6 – RECOVERY

Let's focus on the right way to stand up from the split position with the bar overhead. With your arms locked out overhead, slide your front foot back towards you about halfway. Then, slide your back foot forwards. Repeat this process until your feet are level with each other.

Recovering this way will become important when you are lifting significant weights. Moving your front foot first helps to avoid the weight shifting forwards, which can lead to a missed lift.

STEP 7 – STANDING DIP, DRIVE AND CATCH

For this step, you won't be splitting – we're just going to focus on how we drive the bar up in the first part of the jerk.

Stand with your feet around hip-width apart with the bar in your front rack position. Now, bend your knees to dip into a very shallow squat, keeping your torso vertical and your elbows up. Keep the weight of the bar on your shoulders and your arms relaxed. Quickly straighten your knees to drive the bar upwards. Pull your head back to allow the bar to pass and catch the bar overhead, locking your arms out.

The crucial thing in both of these phases is that the bar moves only vertically. If the bar also moves horizontally (usually forwards), it will be harder to catch it above the head and recover. To drive the bar up vertically, you need to focus on three things:

- Don't allow your elbows to drop in the dip. Keep them in the same position relative to your torso throughout the dip and drive.
- Keep your weight on your heels all the way until the end of the drive – don't roll forwards onto your toes.
- Keep your torso upright. This means that your hips will move downwards during the dip, not backwards.

Dip, drive and catch

If you get these things right, the bar should move vertically and, after it has been driven upwards, should be in a good position to catch it above the shoulders.

STEP 8 - SPLIT JERK

Now you are ready to do the complete jerk movement. Stand like you did for the previous step. Dip and drive the bar overhead but this time, when the bar has passed your face, move quickly into your split position and punch out your arms to catch the bar. Put your head forward so that the bar is over your shoulders.

Finally, recover to standing as you did in step 6 above, moving your front foot first.

Congratulations – you have completed your first split jerk!

COMMON PROBLEM WITH THE SPLIT JERK

Dipping Forward

It is absolutely vital that the bar moves directly upwards in the drive. To achieve that, the dip must also be vertical. If you allow your elbows to drop, roll forward onto your toes or move your torso away from vertical, the bar will move forwards and it will be much harder to complete the rep. You might get away with this with light weights but, as you use heavier weights, you won't be able to save the lift.

Dipping too Deep

While you want to put as much leg drive into the bar as possible, dipping too deep increases the likelihood of dipping forward and can also slow down the drive. You need to experiment to find out what dip depth is right for you but focus more on fast, explosive power rather than depth.

Tight Arms

If you support the weight of the bar on your hands rather than your shoulders or grip the bar too tightly, you will not be able to quickly punch your arms out to catch the bar overhead.

Split too Shallow

It is common for lifters to fail to split deeply enough, especially when using lighter weights. This habit can become a problem when the weights get heavier and a deeper split is required to make the lift. Aim to use a consistent split depth with the front foot ahead of the front knee.

Split too Narrow

You need to maintain shoulder width between your feet. If you allow them to come in from this, you will have too narrow a base, making it more difficult to balance in the split position. Any rotation or instability will be impossible to correct and will cause lifts to be lost.

Not Getting the Head through

As soon as the bar passes your face, you need to push your head forward under the bar. This helps to get the bar over your shoulders where it needs to be.

Weak Lockout

When you punch out your arms overhead to catch the bar, make sure you keep pushing the lockout. If you are at all casual with it, you will struggle with heavier weights.

Loss of Balance on Recovery

If you rush the recovery or recover with you back foot first, you might lose your balance. Be deliberate with the recovery and follow the front foot-back foot-front foot process on every jerk, no matter how light or heavy.

TRAINING THE SPLIT JERK

When you are first learning the jerk, you should do it on its own, either from a rack, from block or by power cleaning the bar first (see chapter 12) in sets of two or three reps.

Once you are confident with both the clean and the jerk, you should train them together, usually in sets of two reps. It can still be useful to train the jerk on its own sometimes though, and many programmes will include jerk-only sessions.

Multiple Rep Sets

If you are doing sets of jerks with multiple reps in them, you will need to return the bar to your shoulders between reps (unless you are using blocks – then you have the option to drop the bar to the blocks between reps).

THE SQUAT JERK

As we mentioned at the start of this chapter, the split jerk is by far the more popular form of jerk – so much so that, when weightlifters just say 'jerk' it is always the split jerk that is being referred to. There is, however, another form of jerk that is used by some lifters in competition. This is the squat jerk, where the lifter drops down into a deep squat rather than splitting under the bar.

Squat jerk catch position

For almost all beginners, the split jerk is the better option but, if you have the mobility for the squat jerk, it would be good to make sure you maintain the ability to perform it.

Challenges

The biggest problem with the squat jerk is the mobility requirement. The receive position is like a snatch receive position with a much narrower grip, with the greater mobility challenges that this presents. Without specific mobility work, most weightlifters will not be able to get into a properly deep receive position and will only be able to perform a power jerk, which may not provide any more depth than a split jerk. Some lifters are trying a wider jerk hand width, which helps with mobility but makes maintaining lockout more challenging.

Assuming you have the mobility to get into a deep squat jerk receive position, the next problem you will face is the very small margin of error. In a split jerk, if the bar is slightly forward or behind the ideal position, it is possible to correct by shifting weight slightly between the feet. In a squat jerk, this is not possible so if the bar is even slightly out of position after the drive, the lift will be lost.

The third challenge of the squat jerk is the tremendous leg strength that is required to complete it. In competition, it will always be attempted immediately after a heavy clean so, in order to be successful, the lifter will need to drive up out of a deep squat twice in quick succession. Especially for beginners, who have not had time to develop the leg strength required, this will limit the weight that can be lifted.

Advantages

So, given all of the difficulties of the squat jerk compared to the split version, why do some lifters use it?

The obvious advantage of a squat jerk over the split variation is that dropping lower means that the bar does not need to be driven so high. Clearly this has the potential to enable bigger weights to be jerked, provided the lifter has the leg strength to stand up out of the deep squat position.

The long drop distance of the squat jerk may give lifters a little more time to achieve a good lockout before their arms take the weight of the bar. For some lifters, this may help avoid missed lifts due to a failed lockout.

Many weightlifters suffer from strength imbalances between their legs, often caused by years of split jerk training. These imbalances can need time-consuming training to rectify. The squat jerk, by its nature, will not induce any imbalance between left and right legs. This could give an advantage to lifters who use the squat variation over many years by enabling them to focus on the lift itself rather than correcting imbalances.

Finally, there are some rare lifters for whom the split jerk just does not click and who find the squat jerk a more natural movement. A warning though – don't leap to the conclusion that the split jerk is not for you on the strength of a few sessions attempting it. It can take several years to master the split jerk, so you will need to persist for some time before assuming it is not for you.

Despite these potential benefits, it is still recommended for beginners to focus on the split jerk. Perhaps the best reason for including the squat jerk initially is that its tight margin of error makes it a good training lift for developing a straight dip and drive.

LEARNING THE SQUAT JERK

Like the split jerk, we talk about the squat jerk in four phases:

- The **dip**, where the lifter bends their legs
- The **drive**, in which the bar is pushed explosively upwards
- The **drop**, where the lifter moves rapidly down into a
  deep squat
- The **recovery** to standing straight.

You should work through the split jerk progression earlier in this chapter to learn the split jerk before trying the squat jerk – that will familiarise you with the dip and drive phases, which work in the same way.

Once you are ready to try the squat version of the jerk, use these steps:

1. Jerk grip overhead squat.
2. Power jerk.
3. Squat jerk.

STEP 1 – JERK GRIP OVERHEAD SQUAT

With the bar in your front rack position, press it up over your head. Now, squat as deep as you can while keeping your arms locked and the bar over your head. You will most likely find this very challenging!

If you are able to get into a deep squat without the bar coming forwards, the squat jerk may be for you. If not, you will need to work on your mobility more. In the meantime, you can use the power jerk as an assistance exercise for the split jerk (see chapter 12).

STEP 2 – POWER JERK

Now, start again with the bar in your front rack position. This time, dip and drive the bar upwards just like you did for the split jerk (see earlier in this chapter). Punch out your arms and catch the bar overhead while dropping into a shallow squat. This is a power jerk.

Power jerk catch position

STEP 3 - SQUAT JERK

The final step of this progression is to catch the bar in a deep squat – the deepest position you were able to get into in the first stage above. You will probably find that you need to moderate the drive and focus more on dropping under the bar in order to catch it at full depth.

PART 4

STRENGTH

"A chain is no stronger than its weakest link."

SIR LESLIE STEPHEN

CHAPTER 10

SQUATS

Aside from snatches, clean and jerks and the various variations, the lifts you will most often see weightlifters performing are squats – descending from an upright position by bending the legs and hips and then returning back up again.

Research consistently shows that squatting with a heavy weight gives all kinds of benefits, both directly in terms of strengthening the muscles that are used and indirectly, such as by encouraging the body to produce more of the hormones that drive muscle growth.

THE BACK SQUAT

Of all of the barbell exercises that are used to build strength, the back squat is probably the most used and the one with the biggest reputation. This reputation is backed up by a lot of evidence from many studies that have shown its benefits.

The back squat forms an important part of the training of almost every Olympic weightlifter. While the front squat arguably transfers better to the requirements of the clean, the back squat enables bigger training loads to be used, driving more adaptation in the body. Most weightlifting training programs include a mix of front and back squats.

HIGH-BAR AND LOW-BAR

If you have done any powerlifting or general barbell strength training, you will probably have come across the low-bar back squat, where the bar is placed on the shoulders, a couple of inches below the neck. For weightlifters, the high-bar back squat, where the bar is placed just below the neck, on the trapezius muscles, is preferred.

High bar (left) and low bar (right) back squats

The high-bar back squat is better for weightlifters because it puts the torso in a position more similar to the competition lifts and enables a deeper squat, so it exercises the range of motion that will be used when catching and recovering from a snatch or clean (at the cost of being a bit more challenging in terms of the weight that can be lifted).

TRANSITIONING FROM POWERLIFTING

If you have a background in powerlifting, you will almost certainly be used to doing a low-bar back squat. Fortunately, it is fairly easy to transition to a high-bar style.

The main thing to aim for is a more vertical torso than you would use for a low-bar back squat. This puts more emphasis on the legs and less on the back, which will transfer to the Olympic movements more directly.

You should also be aiming for a deeper squat than for powerlifting. This may mean that you need to position your feet differently – usually a bit closer together than you would use for a powerlifting squat to parallel.

The main thing to keep in mind is that, unlike in powerlifting, the squat is just an assistance exercise for weightlifters, not a competition lift. Weightlifters tend to benefit more from coming up fast out of squats rather than grinding out slow reps. You may find that you will get better transfer to the Olympic movements if you drop your squat weight in order to move faster.

HOW TO BACK SQUAT

The back squat is always performed using a squat rack or a power cage (see chapter 2). Before you start, get the bar at the right height so that you can lift it out of the rack easily without needing to stretch upwards. If the rack or cage has safety bars, remove them for now or set them to their lowest height – you will not need them with just the bar.

Dip your head under the bar and position it across the top of your shoulders, just under your neck. If you push your shoulders backwards, you should feel a shelf formed by your trapezius muscles – rest the bar on this. Grip the bar but make sure the weight of the bar is on your shoulders, not your hands.

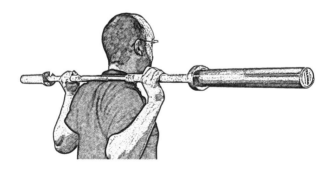

High bar back squat bar position

Straighten your legs to lift the bar out of the rack and take a step backwards. Position your feet at about shoulder-width apart with your toes pointing slightly outwards. The right foot width and position to use can take a bit of experimentation – everyone is different. As a starting point, use the same foot position that you have in the snatch catch position.

Now, take a big breath in, hold it in and push to make the core of your body feel tight. This tightness is really important when you start adding weight to the back squat so you need to learn to maintain it on every rep.

When your core is locked tight, slowly squat down, bending your knees and pushing your hips backwards. Keep your weight mid-foot and don't allow your chest to drop. The aim is for the bar to descend vertically so that it stays over your feet. If you have anything less than perfect mobility, you will probably find that, at some point, you won't be able to squat any lower without the bar moving forwards so that it is no longer over your feet. Stop when you reach this point. This is your back squat bottom position, at least until you improve your mobility.

Back squat

Now, push through your feet, straighten your legs and bring your hips forward to return to your standing position. You have completed one rep of the back squat.

COMMON PROBLEMS WITH THE BACK SQUAT

Before you start adding lots of weight to your back squat, you need to make sure you are using good form. If you don't have access to a good coach, record yourself squatting from different angles and watch out for these commonly seen issues.

Sometimes, these problems will not be apparent with an empty bar so, when you do start adding weight, continue the process of analysing your form and correcting any issues that show themselves.

Losing Tightness in Your Back and Core

It is vital that you maintain a good tight back in a neutral position. Before each set of squats, get your back set and take a big breath in to help to keep your core tight (see chapter 4) and maintain this tightness throughout every rep. If you need to breathe between reps, make sure you get your core tight.again.

Heels Coming Up

You want to keep all parts of your feet down throughout each squat rep. If you find that you just can't keep your heels down no matter how hard you try, you have a mobility problem that you need to address (see chapter 3).

Leaning Forward

Dipping forwards from the hips during a squat rep is sometimes called a 'squat morning' in reference to the 'good morning' exercise where you bow forwards at the waist. The problem with doing this is that you move the weight of the bar further forward, creating a longer lever length and thus more force on your back.

This can be caused either by a mobility problem or by a strength disparity between legs and back – lifters with strong backs will often do this to complete heavier squat reps than they would otherwise be able to. For weightlifting, we want to be building strength in a good position, so if you find yourself dipping forwards, drop the weight slightly and get good reps in.

Knees Coming Inwards

We want the knees to track out in line with the feet to avoid twisting forces. If you find your knees drifting inwards during squats even with light weights you probably have a mobility issue to address. If this only happens as the load is increased, the cause is more likely a weakness of some kind. A good exercise for this is to do light squats with a resistance band around the knees, focusing on keeping the knees tracking in line with the feet.

Dropping too Fast

You want the descent of your squats to be fully under control. This means you have to keep your muscles fully engaged rather than just allowing the weight to make you drop too fast, which is sometimes called 'dive bombing'.

TRAINING THE BACK SQUAT

There are many different approaches to training the squat. For weightlifting, typically sets of between three and six reps are used, with around twelve to twenty works reps in a session. So that might be 3 x 6, 4 x 5, 5 x 3 or some other combination.

In addition to your work sets, once you start putting serious weight on the bar, you will also need to do some warm-up sets. The number of warm-ups will depend on how heavy your work sets will be but for most beginner and intermediate lifters, three to four warm-up sets will be sufficient.

For example, if you plan to squat 100kg for four sets of five, you might do the following warm-up:

- Bar (20kg) - 5 reps
- 40kg - 5 reps
- 60kg - 4 reps
- 80kg - 3 reps

The exact weights and reps that you do are not crucial – the important thing is that you work up to your work weight steadily and without doing so much work that your work sets are affected.

THE FRONT SQUAT

It's not surprising that the front squat is an important training exercise for weightlifters – the recovery part of the clean movement is essentially the concentric (upward) part of a front squat.

The clean recovery

A common rule of thumb is that a lifter should be capable of cleaning a weight that they can front squat for a set of three reps. This assumes very good technique on the clean, so if you are not fully efficient on the clean yet, you will need to be able to front squat somewhat more.

Compared to the back squat, the front squat is more challenging in terms of the weight that can be used. This is because the more upright front squat does not enable the big muscles of the posterior chain (the back and the back of the legs) to contribute so much to moving the weight. Instead, the quadriceps on the front of the leg has to work harder.

HOW TO FRONT SQUAT

As with the back squat, you should use a rack or power cage for the front squat. You will need to place the bar a bit lower than you did for the back squat.

Approach the bar with your knees slightly bent, making sure you are centred on it. Position the middle of the bar just under your neck and place you hands on the bar just wider than your shoulders. Now, rotate your elbows under the bar into front rack position.

Rack position

Now, straighten your legs to lift the bar out of the rack and take a step backwards. Position your feet about shoulder-width apart, pointing slightly outwards.

Front squat start position

Bend your knees and squat down, keeping your elbows up and your torso as vertical as possible. Descend as deep as you can without your elbows dropping or your back rounding.

Front squat bottom position

Push through your heels, straighten your legs and return to the position you started from.

COMMON PROBLEMS WITH THE FRONT SQUAT

All of the problems described earlier in this chapter for the back squat can occur in the front squat, so take another look at that section.

In addition, because of the position of the bar on the front of the shoulders, in a front squat dropping the elbows can lead to serious rounding of the upper back. If this happens, it is a sign that you are attempting too heavy a weight.

Goblet squats (see later in this chapter) are a good exercise for improving your front squat position. If this is something you need to work on, it is a good idea to do a few sets of goblet squats as a warm-up for front squats.

TRAINING THE FRONT SQUAT

Compared to the back squat, we tend to use a lower rep range in the front squat. Sets of three are the most common way to programme the majority of front squat work.

As with the back squat, you need to do a few warm-up sets to work up to your work weight.

THE GOBLET SQUAT

This squat is often overlooked as, due to its nature, you can't use a huge weight for it. However, it is a fantastic way to practise the correct posture and mobility for the bigger squatting movements, especially front squats.

Grab a kettlebell or dumbbell – start light and work up. Hold it in front of you, just under your chin. Now, with your feet about shoulder-width apart, squat down as deep as you can.

Goblet Squat

Since goblet squats are not performed with big weights, it is good to do them slowly, focusing on getting into a really good, deep position. It is even good to pause for a few seconds at the bottom of the movement – by doing this, the goblet squat can act as a stretch to improve mobility.

THE OVERHEAD SQUAT

We used the overhead squat as part of the progression for learning the snatch. It forms part of the warm-up for snatch for most lifters. It can also be a useful training lift with some weight on, to focus on stability in the overhead position.

Overhead squat

CHAPTER 11

PRESSES

F or weightlifters, presses are movements that involve using the arms to push the weight above the head. We don't want to use the arms to push the weight up in the Olympic movements (indeed, in a competition, that would be an illegal lift) but it is still important to develop strength in the arms in order to be able to lock out a heavy weight overhead. Presses also help with developing good shoulder strength, which is important for stability and injury prevention.

Presses are usually trained with sets of between three and eight reps.

STRICT PRESS

The most basic press is the strict press, also sometimes known as the military or mil press. In this movement, just the shoulders and arms are used to move the weight.

Stand with your feet about hip-width apart with the bar on the front of your shoulders, similar to where you would have it for a front squat.

Strict press start position

Unlike in the front rack position you use for front squats and cleans, you must ensure you have a full grip on the bar for presses. Also, you should drop your elbows so that your forearms are close to vertical, rather than in the high position of the front rack.

Now, take a big breath in and lock your core. At the same time squeeze your glutes and tense your quads – this will help stabilise your body during the movement. Keep your weight on your heels.

When you are ready, push the bar upwards off your shoulders. You will need to move your head backwards slightly to enable the bar to come past.

Strict press - bar passing face

As soon as the bar is past your face, move your head forwards again so that the bar is above you shoulders. Keep straightening your arms until they are locked out.

Strict press - finish position

Hold the bar in the lockout position for a short time and then reverse the process to return the bar to the shoulders. During the downwards part of the movement, known as the eccentric phase, don't just let the bar drop – make it descend slowly and under control.

If you need to breathe during a set of presses, do so when the bar is overhead and your arms are locked out. If you try to breathe while the bar is on your shoulders, the upper back will tend to round somewhat.

PUSH PRESS

One you are confident with the strict press, you can move on to the push press. You will now be using some leg power to help push the bar up. Obviously this means you should be able to push press significantly more weight than you can strict press. This dip and drive movement also transfers directly to the jerk.

Use the same start position as you would for a jerk, making sure the weight of the bar is on your shoulders, not your hands.

Start the push press by bending your knees to dip slightly. You should keep your weight on your heels and your torso vertical. Then, explosively straighten your legs to drive the bar upwards, just like you would for a jerk. You are aiming to use the maximum amount of leg power and the minimum of arm strength. If you do it right, you should only need to engage your shoulders and arms to lock out once the bar is above your head.

The push press

SNATCH GRIP PRESS

Both the strict press and the push press can be performed using a snatch grip. In this case, the bar is placed on the back of the shoulders rather than the front. The rest of the techniques are the same (apart from the fact that you don't need to move your head back out of the way of the bar).

SNATCH GRIP SOTS PRESS

One of the most challenging pressing movements is the Sots press, where a press is performed while in a deep squat. Originally, pressing in a deep squat was named after Russian weightlifter Viktor Sots, who pressed from the front as an assistance exercise for squat jerks. However, over the years the name has been increasingly used for any kind of press from a deep squat and the snatch grip version is more widely used.

Snatch grip Sots press

The Sots press is most often used as a warm-up for snatch or as a mobility exercise – very rarely is it loaded with significant weight due to the risks of doing so in such a difficult position.

CHAPTER 12

DEADLIFTS

In some ways, the deadlift is the simplest barbell movement of all – the weight is lifted up from the floor and then put back down again. It is certainly right up there in terms of the movements that enable the most weight to be lifted.

The downside of the large loads that can be used for deadlifts is fatigue – both of muscles and the central nervous system. Fatigue can have a big impact on the speed and power required for the Olympic lifts, so weightlifters don't tend to deadlift with anywhere near maximal weights. For weightlifters, the deadlifts are assistance exercises which help us to maintain good positions when lifting the bar.

Many weightlifters have little or no deadlifting in their training programmes. Deadlifts tend to be used as required to address specific issues and weaknesses.

GRIP AND STRAPS

It is very common for lifters to use straps (see chapter 2) for deadlifts to make it easier to grip the bar. It is certainly a good idea to use straps if your hands are suffering from too much bar work. However, consider doing at least warm-up sets without straps – deadlifts are great exercises for building your grip strength and it would be a shame to miss out.

SNATCH GRIP DEADLIFT

If you have difficulty with the first pull in the snatch or if you struggle to maintain a strong, tight back during the lift, the snatch grip deadlift could be a good assistance exercise for you.

HOW TO SNATCH GRIP DEADLIFT

In a snatch grip deadlift, you want to replicate the movement pattern of the first parts of a snatch, so start off in the same position you would use for a snatch.

Snatch grip deadlift start position

Then, use your legs to lift the bar off the platform. Your knees will come back, enabling the bar to rise up vertically and pass the knees.

Snatch grip deadlift - bar at knees

As the weight will be heavier in a deadlift than you would use for a snatch, focus extra hard on keeping your chest up and a strong, tight back.

Now, bring the bar up the thighs and into the hips. Keep your arms long and loose throughout the movement and keep your weight balanced between the balls of your feet and your heels.

Snatch grip deadlift - bar at hips

This is the point where in a snatch or a snatch pull, you would explosively drive the bar upwards. Instead, just straighten your legs to lock them out. This is the finish position of the deadlift.

Deadlift finish position

Now, you want to return the bar to the platform by reversing the movement you used to lift it. This downward or 'eccentric' part of the movement is a valuable part of the exercise for building strength, so don't be tempted to drop the weight. Keep your back tight all the way until the bar is back on the platform.

When performing multiple reps of the snatch grip deadlift, don't bounce the bar off the platform between reps. Return the bar to the platform, reset yourself and then start the next rep. Deadlifts should start from a dead stop each and every time!

CLEAN GRIP DEADLIFT

The clean grip deadlift fills the same role for the clean as the snatch grip deadlift does for the snatch. It can help to solve problems with pulling the weight off the platform or with maintaining positions. It can also help psychologically by getting you used to lifting heavier weights from the platform.

TRANSITIONING FROM POWERLIFTING

While the clean grip deadlift may seem superficially very similar to the deadlift used by powerlifters, there are actually some important differences.

Firstly, you may deadlift barefoot or in deadlift slippers for training a powerlifting style deadlift. When using the clean grip deadlift as an assistance exercise for the clean, you want to be wearing your weightlifting shoes.

For a clean grip deadlift, we start in the exact same position that we would use to start a clean. This almost certainly means that your hips will be lower than they would be for a powerlifting deadlift and your knees will be bent more.

In a clean grip deadlift, we want to replicate the movement pattern of the clean as closely as possible. That means that we want to stay over the bar for longer than we would if we were just trying to deadlift a maximal weight.

The final difference is the kind of loading that we use – Olympic weightlifters very rarely want to subject themselves to the high CNS load of maximal deadlifts, so tend to work at much lower intensities than would be used by powerlifters who are focusing on the deadlift as a competition lift.

HOW TO CLEAN GRIP DEADLIFT

Start in the same position you would use to start a clean.

Clean grip deadlift - start position

Engage your legs to bring the bar up to the knees, which should have moved back to enable it to pass. Keep your back tight, your chest up and your arms long and loose.

Clean grip deadlift - bar at knees

Then, bring the bar to mid-thigh, maintaining your tight back, loose arms and keeping your weight distributed evenly between the balls of your feet and your heels.

Clean grip deadlift - bar at hips

Finally, complete the movement by standing vertically and locking your legs out.

Deadlift finish position

Return the bar to the platform by reversing these movements. As described earlier for the snatch grip deadlift, complete this part of the movement under control and maintaining a tight back.

HALTING/SEGMENT DEADLIFT

Both snatch and clean grip deadlifts can be performed using a halting movement. These are also known as segment deadlifts.

Pausing at key positions helps to make sure you are getting them right and can also focus on making you stronger in positions where you are currently relatively weak.

DEFICIT DEADLIFT

In the deficit version of a snatch or clean grip deadlift, you stand on a short block (normally around one or two inches high) so that you are lifting the bar from below the height you are standing at. This makes the lift more challenging and can develop more strength in the initial pull from the platform.

It is important to make sure you are maintaining a flat back in deficit lifts. Some lifters who are able to get a good flat back in the normal start position struggle in the deficit start position, especially if the block used is too high.

ROMANIAN DEADLIFT

Although this exercise shares a similar name to the snatch and clean grip deadlifts, it is actually a very different kind of exercise. The Romanian deadlift, or RDL as is it often known, starts with the lifter standing up with the bar and involves little movement in the legs.

The Romanian deadlift got its name from Nicu Vlad, a multiple world champion and Olympic gold medallist, who used the movement primarily to build back strength for the clean. Since he did not have a name for it, when others followed him in doing it, they called it the Romanian deadlift.

Romanian deadlifts are great for building back and hamstring strength.

HOW TO ROMANIAN DEADLIFT

Start with holding the bar with a clean grip and deadlifting the bar up so that you are standing vertically. Then, bend your knees slightly. This is the start position for the RDL.

Romanian deadlift start position

Through the rest of the movement, you should not bend your knees any more than they are in the start position.

Now, pivot at your hips to slowly bring the bar down your legs, keeping your knees fixed at the angle they are at.

Romanian deadlift - partway down

Keep your back tight to prevent any rounding. You should start to feel some tightness in your hamstrings as the bar gets lower down your legs. If you don't, it's likely that you are bending your knees too much.

When you can't lower the bar any further without bending your knees, you have reached the bottom position.

Romanian deadlift - bottom position

Now, lift the bar back to the start position, again keeping the angle of the knees fixed.

If you managed to lower the bar all the way to the platform during the rep, check that you are not bending at your knees more than a very small amount and that you are not rounding your back. If neither of these things is happening, congratulations – you have great mobility! You can stand on a small block to enable a slightly bigger range of motion.

Romanian deadlift on a block

CHAPTER 13

CORE STRENGTH AND STABILITY

W e use the biggest muscles of our body to do most of the work in weightlifting but the smaller muscles are important too. These muscles perform important roles in enabling us to maintain good positions. They are also vital for keeping us stable – protecting our joints from twisting forces that could lead to injury.

The most common area that is talked about is 'the core' – the muscles around the lower torso and especially the abdominals. However, we also need to pay attention to the muscles around the shoulders that are critical for safely holding heavy weights overhead.

All of the other strength exercises that we have talked about will make use of these muscles and so will train them but it is a good idea to do some work that specifically targets them.

There are a huge number of exercises that you can do to address core strength and stability. In this chapter, we will look at some of the most common that are used by weightlifters.

Usually these exercises will be done at the end of training sessions or separately on rest days. They are often done as a circuit, moving straight from one exercise to another.

PLANKS

To do a basic plank, lie down and push yourself up so your weight is supported by your elbows, forearms and feet.

Plank

The crucial thing to get right in order to do the exercise properly is to keep your whole body lined up so your back is flat and your legs are straight.

You should aim to hold this position for at least thirty seconds. You may find that to start with this is challenging – if so, just hold for as long as you can. If you do planks regularly, you will be able to hold them for longer but the evidence seems to show that holding planks for longer than around a minute gives little additional benefit so once you reach that point, you are probably better off starting to do weighted planks (see below) rather than pushing for longer holds.

SIDE PLANKS

While the basic plank is a great exercise, it's good to do some variations to target slightly different sets of muscles around the core. To do a side plank, support yourself on one elbow and foot facing sideways.

Side plank

As with the basic plank, focus on keeping your body straight (both horizontally and vertically).

Repeat the exercise on each side, holding for thirty second to a minute on each side.

WEIGHTED PLANKS

When basic planks become too easy, you can add weight by getting someone to place weight plates on your back.

Weighted plank

Make sure the plates are positioned securely midway up your back.

As with basic planks, aim to hold the position for thirty seconds to a minute.

ABDOMINAL ROLLOUTS

For an exercise that is similar to a plank but with a dynamic element, kneel on the floor with a loaded barbell in front of you. Grip the barbell at about shoulder width and roll it away from you, supporting your weight on your hands and knees. Go as far forward as you can while still being able to return to your original position.

Do these for a few sets of eight to ten reps.

LEG RAISES

Use a pull-up bar or other convenient bar for this exercise. Grab the bar and raise your legs in front of you.

Leg raise

Don't swing or use momentum to help you lift your legs – to get the maximum benefit, you want to raise them slowly and under complete control.

FEET TO BAR

For a more advanced version of leg raises, aim to raise your feet all the way to the bar above you.

Feet to bar

STANDING TWIST

This is another simple exercise that builds your ability to work with twisting forces. Hold a weight plate in front of you and twist at the waist, first one way and then the other.

Standing twist

Go slowly – this exercise is not about getting the reps done as quickly as possible.

SAXON SIDE BEND

Stand with a dumbbell in each hand overhead and bend to the side, one way and then the other.

Saxon side bend

Keep your movements slow and controlled and make sure you are not bending forwards or backwards.

OVERHEAD HOLDS

For overhead stability, a good exercise is to press a barbell overhead (see chapter 9) and hold it there, keeping your body upright.

Overhead hold

You will find that this will become challenging after a short while, even with a low weight on the bar. Keep your legs, glutes, core, back, shoulders and arms tight and drop the bar when your body starts shaking too much to keep the weight stable overhead.

Another option is to do a handstand against a wall and hold the position for as long as possible with your arms locked.

PART 5

POWER

"Pull the bar like you're ripping the head off of a lion"

DONNY SHANKLE

CHAPTER 14

POWER VARIATIONS

The snatch, clean and jerk all have a power variation that puts more emphasis on driving the bar high rather than on dropping deep underneath it.

All of the power variations are actually legal to use in competition – there is no requirement to sit in deep, although obviously most lifters can get bigger lifts by catching the bar deep. Some lifters (especially masters lifters) who don't have the mobility to squat deep will use a power snatch or a power clean. Sometimes, lifters who have not developed a great jerk yet will power clean rather than clean because they want to save the maximum leg power for the jerk. If possible though, most lifters should use the full depth variations as the limiting factor will eventually be how high they can pull the bar, so using full depth gives potential for bigger lifts.

For training purposes, these assistance lifts are useful for focusing on extending fully in the second pull of the snatch and clean. For the jerk, the focus is on a strong, vertical drive in the jerk. Power variations also have to be completed at high speed, so they are good if that is something that you need to improve on.

Another reason why power variations of the snatch and clean are included in weightlifting training programmes is that they tend to cause smaller central nervous system and fatigue loads, as the recovery component of the lift is much shorter and the loads are usually lower.

For beginners it is often wise to avoid training the power variations a lot, at least to start with. If you practise catching the bar in a high position, it can make it more difficult to learn to sit in and catch deep.

POWER SNATCH

You begin a power snatch just like you would a snatch. Everything up to the second pull is exactly the same.

The difference comes in how deep you squat to catch the bar. Technically, anything caught above parallel (the point where your thighs are parallel to the platform) is a power snatch.

When you use the power snatch as an assistance exercise, you want to focus on extending fully in the second pull. This is often referred to as 'finishing the pull'.

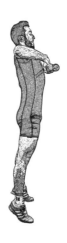

Snatch extension

It is also good to use the power snatch as an opportunity to work on how you distribute your weight on your feet. You want to try to keep your weight centred on your feet as long as possible. You will come up onto your toes as a result of the pull, but you don't want to roll onto the toes too early.

You should be fully extended, as tall as possible, before dropping under. By doing this, you will be able to catch the bar as high as possible.

Even though you will not be dropping down into a full-depth squat, you still want to squat to catch the bar. A common mistake in a power snatch is to 'starfish' – keeping the legs straight but jumping the feet out wider to drop under the bar. Don't do this. Instead, use the same foot width that you would for a full-depth snatch and just squat a bit shallower.

A key skill to develop to be good at power snatch and power clean is to drop just deep enough to catch the bar and then lock your whole body tight to prevent the weight of the bar from pushing you deeper.

Once you have caught the bar, stand upright to complete the movement.

Many beginner lifters can power snatch as much as they can snatch, some-times even a bit more. This is because the shallower squat used in the power snatch is a more stable position. The power snatch is also a little more forgiving of the bar being a bit forward. As you improve, you should find that you are able to lift more weight with a full snatch. Most experi-enced weightlifters power snatch around 85% of their full snatch.

POWER CLEAN

Just like with the power snatch, you should approach the start of a power clean just as you would a full clean. Lift the bar from the platform in just the same way but, when it reaches mid-thigh, use maximal force to extend and pull the bar as high as possible.

Clean extension

You need to approach a power clean catch with a different mentality from that which you would use for a full clean. In a full clean, you want to bring the bar to just the right height to catch it in a deep squat. In a power clean you want to catch it as high as possible.

Power clean catch position

When doing a power clean, you will have to be even faster to whip your elbows through under the bar than you would be for a full clean. You don't want the bar to drop at all before you catch it and lock tight.

As with the power snatch, use the same feet width for the catch as you would in the full-depth version of the lift and lock your whole body tight when you catch the bar, before standing upright.

Most experienced lifters can power clean around 85% of their full clean. It is not unusual for beginners to be able to power clean as much as they can clean. If this is the case, you need to work on dropping under the bar faster in the full clean.

POWER JERK

Assuming, like most people, you use the split jerk, you will find the power jerk a little different from your usual jerk, as it has more in common with the squat jerk (see chapter 7) In a power jerk, rather than splitting, you will drop into a shallow squat to catch the bar overhead.

Dip and drive just as you would for a split jerk but, when the bar passes your face, jump your feet out slightly, to around shoulder width, and squat into about a quarter squat, while punching your arms out to catch the bar.

Power jerk catch position

One thing that you will quickly discover is that you need to be very disciplined with your dip and drive on power jerks. In a split jerk, if the bar goes slightly forward in the drive, it is possible to rescue the lift by shifting more weight onto the front foot. Because your feet are side by side in a power jerk, you don't have this option – if the bar is in front of you, you will probably miss the lift. Along with speed and power required to drive the bar higher, it is this smaller margin of error on the dip and drive that makes the power jerk such a useful training exercise, even if you use the split jerk normally.

To ensure the dip and drive are vertical, you will have to remember the key points that we discussed in chapter 7 – don't drop your elbows, keep your weight on your heels and your torso upright.

Experienced lifters will power jerk around 90% of their clean and jerk weight.

CHAPTER 15

PULLS

O ne of the key things that determines whether you will make a snatch or clean is the ability to pull the weight high enough to get under the bar. Getting stronger with the exercises that we looked at in the last section will help with this but, because they tend to be performed more slowly than the competition lifts, they don't focus on developing the power that is need for a really good pull. This chapter looks at pulls – as the name implies, these exercises replicate the pulls of the snatch and clean and are fantastic ways to get better at this part of the lifts.

Later in this chapter, we also look at the jerk drive, which is not strictly speaking a pull but fulfils the same role for the jerk as the pulls do for the snatch and clean.

Pulls and jerk drives are usually trained with a bit more weight than would be used for the full lifts that they are aimed at assisting. As well as helping us to get stronger for the main lifts, the extra weight can be useful for gaining confidence and generally getting used to the feel of heavier loads.

SNATCH PULL

Like the power snatch that we looked at in the previous chapter, the snatch pull begins just like a full snatch. Everything up until the second pull should be exactly the same. The difference is that in a snatch pull, we don't attempt to get under the bar at all: the movement is complete when we reach full extension in the second pull.

Snatch extension

Even more so than with the power snatch, the emphasis should be on finishing really tall in the pull. For a standard snatch pull, your arms should remain relaxed throughout the movement – they will bend as the momentum of the bar carries it upwards from the second pull but you should not actively engage your arms to pull the bar higher. See below for some variations that are different in this regard.

Another thing to focus on when doing snatch pulls is keeping the bar close to you. Because you will not be dropping under the bar, you can concentrate on ensuring that the bar rises as vertically as possible and thus stays close to your body.

VARIATIONS OF THE SNATCH PULL

There are several variations of the snatch pull that are used to alter the focus of the exercise to some extent. As a beginner, it is best to save these for later but a coach, if you have one, may prescribe one or more of these variations for you, so it is good to know the differences between them.

High Snatch Pull

In this version, when the bar reaches the top of the second pull, you engage your arms to pull the bar even higher, while maintaining the tall position of the standard snatch pull.

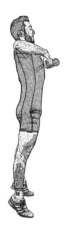

Snatch high pull

Halting/Segment Snatch Pull

If you need to work more on your intermediate positions, your coach may ask you to pause at one or more of the key positions of the lift during snatch pulls.

Deficit Snatch Pull

If you need to get stronger at the very first part of the lift, standing on a low block for snatch pulls can help.

Deficit snatch pull

This makes the movement more challenging, so use less weight.

Speed Pull/Fast Pull/Snatch Pull Down/Panda Pull

The fact that no standard name for this variation has been agreed on is probably due to the fact that its use is fairly rare. It's a development of the high snatch pull where the lifter pulls themself down into a squat at the end of the pull. It can be useful for advanced lifters but we would recommend avoiding it unless you have a specific reason for using it – for beginner and intermediate lifters, it is much better to focus on full extension when doing snatch pulls.

CLEAN PULL

The clean pull works in the same way as the snatch pull – you treat it just like a power clean but you don't drop under the bar at all.

Clean extension

Really focus on finishing in a tall, fully extended position and keeping the arms long and loose to enable the bar to move vertically, close to your body.

VARIATIONS OF THE CLEAN PULL

The clean pull has most of the same variations as the snatch pull. As with the snatch pull, these variations are used for specific purposes – as a beginner, it is best to stick to the standard version.

High Clean Pull

This variation is often used by athletes from other sports who want to develop explosive power without developing the technique required for the Olympic lifts. It can also be useful for intermediate weightlifters, to focus on engaging the arms straight after the second pull.

Halting/Segment Clean Pull

Sometimes a coach will instruct you to pause at one or more key positions during a clean pull. Doing this puts the focus on those positions and enables a coach to ensure your positions are perfect.

Deficit Clean Pull

Standing on a low block will make the very first part of the lift more challenging and so can be useful if this is something that you need to improve.

JERK DRIVE

The jerk drive is the equivalent of the pulls for working on being more powerful during the drive phase of the jerk.

To do a jerk drive, approach it in exactly the same way as a jerk but, after the bar comes up off your shoulders, just step back and allow it to drop in front of you.

Jerk drive

Jerk drives are almost always done using jerk blocks because the bar is dropped between each rep.

When doing jerk drives, really focus on using the maximum amount of leg power as quickly as possible to push the bar upwards and off your shoulders. At the same time, make sure you are driving upwards vertically – the bar should not be moving forwards at all.

CHAPTER 16

PLYOMETRICS

'Plyometrics' (at least nowadays) is usually a fancy way to say 'jumping'. The original theory of plyometrics was based on exercises that stretch the muscles (the name comes from the Greek *plëa* meaning 'more'). Originally these exercises involved a drop (like the depth jump that we look at later in this chapter) but over time, the term has come to include all kinds of jumping exercises.

These exercises are useful for training to be as fast as possible at moving a sub-maximal weight. That will transfer to the Olympic lifts, especially if speed is something that you struggle with.

Some of the plyometric exercises can also be useful for gauging fatigue levels while following a training programme. Increases in fatigue will usually lead to a drop in performance in jumping exercises, so doing some vertical jumps or standing long jumps at the start of each training session and recording the results can be a good way to assess the effect that training is having.

VERTICAL JUMP

The simplest of all the jumps and the one that is most obviously similar to the vertical propulsion that is used in the Olympic lifts is the vertical jump.

Stand with your feet about hip-width apart (the same width you would use to start a snatch or clean). Have your arms up in front of you.

Vertical jump start position

Bend at your knees and hips to dip down. The best depth to use is individual so you will need to experiment to see what gives you the best height.

Vertical jump dip

Now explosively straighten your knees and hips to jump upwards as high as possible.

Vertical jump extension

Land in a shallow squat to cushion the impact.

Vertical jump landing

You can measure your vertical jumps by standing next to a wall and reaching your arms upwards (don't stretch, just put them above your head) and marking the height of the hand nearer to the wall (a little chalk on the fingertips is useful for this). Then jump and touch the wall as high as possible – the difference between the two marks is your vertical jump height.

Another way to use vertical jumps is in a set, where you immediately jump again as soon as you land, keeping your contact time with the floor to a minimum. This introduces stretch reflex in the same way as a depth jump (see later) and can be a really good warm-up exercise before weightlifting training.

BOX JUMP

The technique for a box jump is very similar to the vertical jump. The difference is that this time, you are jumping up onto a block, landing in a squat position.

Box jump

You can vary this exercise by using different squat heights in the landing position. Common variations are a ninety-degree knee angle or landing in the position you would use for the dip during a jerk.

Box jumps can be potentially dangerous so it is very important to make sure that the blocks that you use are stable and to work up gradually with progressively higher blocks. Also, don't overlook the hazards of getting down from the block – either step down carefully or jump down and reduce the impact on your legs by landing in a squat.

DEPTH JUMP

In a depth jump, the idea is to trigger the stretch reflex in your muscles by jumping down from a height and springing straight back up with minimum contact time with the floor.

Stand on a block and jump down onto the floor. As you land, dip into a shallow squat and immediately jump upwards. Try to make the time that your feet are touching the floor as short as possible. Don't try to jump back onto the block – just jump as high as you can in the air.

As with box jumps, work your way up gradually. This is a high-impact exercise that should be treated with caution.

STANDING LONG JUMP

Unlike the other jumps, in this one you are aiming to propel yourself horizontally (although to reach the maximum distance, some vertical propulsion is needed too).

Stand with your feet hip–width apart and your arms raised. Bend your knees and hips to bend down and simultaneously lower your arms. Then, explosively extend while rolling forwards onto your toes to jump forwards.

You will need to experiment a bit to find the launch angle that gives you the best distance.

Because it is relatively easy to measure consistently, the standing long jump has been used in lots of research, which has found strong links between it and overall athletic performance. For this reason, it is often used to assess sporting potential.

PART 6

DISCIPLINE

"I was never talented and nobody will call me talented, I am just a workaholic."

DMITRY KLOKOV

CHAPTER 17

WEIGHTLIFTING TRAINING

Like any really interesting skill, it takes most people a long time to get good at weightlifting. Even once you have a good basic technique, you are going to have to train frequently in order to keep consistent while hitting new personal bests.

The fact that weightlifting is so hard is both the best and most frustrating thing about it. There is a fantastic sense of satisfaction from making a new best lift and, at the start, this will happen often. However, as you lifter closer and closer to your strength potential, these moments require longer and longer periods of dedicated training.

To get to the very highest level in weightlifting requires a huge amount of dedication and the ability to train even when you are feeling tired and in pain. As a beginner, though, that lies a long way in the future. For now, you should focus on developing your mobility, technique, strength and power incrementally – small improvements will add up to big changes over time.

WEIGHTLIFTING ALONGSIDE OTHER SPORTS

It's becoming increasingly common for the Olympic weightlifting movements to be used by athletes whose main focus in on another sport. If you are just looking to use the Olympic lifts to improve your power for jumping, throwing, sprinting or general athleticism, your training will be very different from what a full-time weightlifter would do. Often in this situation, you will want to focus on the power variations and pulls more than the full lifts.

If you train for CrossFit®, it is important that you develop good, efficient Olympic weightlifting movements. While you will not be able to devote all of your time to them, spending some time improving your technique will pay dividends during tough weightlifting-focused WODs.

TRAINING AT A CLUB OR GYM

Every club has its own culture and etiquette, so when starting to train somewhere new it is a good idea to find out what the expectations are. Some rules are almost universal though:

- If someone is already using a platform, ask if they mind you joining them - they should say yes but it is polite to ask
- Stay well clear when anyone else is lifting
- Don't walk across a platform except when you go onto your platform to lift
- Load and unload your own bar
- Use the minimum number of plates required to make the weight you need
- When you are done, unload your bar and return the bar and plates to the proper place
- It is normal to have a moment of quiet when someone is attempting a personal best
- Don't use the best bars for doing squats or other assistance exercises - most gyms have some older or lower quality bars for that

THE TRAINING SESSION

Weightlifting training sessions usually last between one and three hours. Absolute beginners tend to do best when the sessions are kept quite short while advanced and elite lifters need more time to recover between sets of heavy lifts and will also be doing more assistance exercises.

When you are just getting started, you will be using light weights and focusing on technique, so you will be able to train often – even every day if time allows. As you add weight to your lifts, you will soon find that you need some recovery time between training sessions, meaning that training more than three or four times a week is counter-productive. More advanced lifters who have adapted to regular lifting will train more often – even multiple times in a day.

Almost every weightlifter gets the best results by following a training programme which specifies how many times to train each week and what to do during each session. When choosing a programme or agreeing one with a coach, it is important to think about how many times you will be able to train – there's no point committing to a five-session-a-week programme if you will only be able to make it to the gym three times.

WHEN TO TRAIN

For most people, training in the afternoon or early evening is ideal – mobility is generally better than in the morning and the central nervous system is firing well. However, the reality for most lifters is that we have to fit training into our lifestyles, so if you have to train first thing in the morning or late at night, you can make it work.

If you have to train early in the morning, it is a good idea to do some extra mobility work before starting your main exercises. You may also find that you need to do a few more warm up sets with light weights to get your CNS firing and your technique locked in.

TRAINING PARTNERS

Who you train with can make a huge difference to how much you get out of your time in the gym. You want to be working alongside lifters who will motivate you to get the best out of yourself. Usually this means training with lifters who are a bit more experienced but the most important thing is to find like minded people.

WORKING WITH A COACH

As we mentioned in chapter 2, it is important to find a coach who is the right fit for you. There are as many coaching styles as there are coaches so if your first choice doesn't work well for you, don't be afraid to find someone else. On the other hand, don't fall into the trap of blaming all difficulties on the wrong kind of coaching - it takes time to make progress so flitting from coach to coach may be counter-productive. Give it time before switching.

While working with a coach, try to resist the temptation to take advice from too many other people. If you make drastic changes to your technique based on input from elsewhere, it will make things more difficult for your own coach. If you come across an idea you would like to try, discuss it with your coach first before implementing it.

If you are following a programme given to you by your coach, try to follow it as closely as you can. If you don't there will be no way to know whether the programme is working for you or not. The reality is that there will be times when you can't follow the programme to the letter, often because of time or equipment restrictions. Make sure to let your coach know if that happens - they may want to adjust the programme to suit you better.

Give your coach as much feedback as you can on your training - the more information they have, the better they can help you. This is particularly true if you experience any pain - keeping quiet can lead to a niggle becoming an injury when it could have been easily prevented with some adjustments.

The most important thing is to trust your coach. They may ask you to focus on particular things that seem unimportant but they will be using all of their experience to guide you in the right direction.

PREPARATION

For most of us who have limited time to train each week, the time we spend in the gym is precious. It makes sense, then, to do what we can to make the most of the time we have. There are some simple things you can do before even going to the gym that will help maximise the value you get from your training time.

One of the biggest things that can affect performance in the Olympic lifts, especially when learning new techniques, is tiredness. Getting a good night's sleep before training days can make a huge difference.

Make sure you are well hydrated ahead of training. Ideally, you should be drinking plenty of water all the time but pay special attention to it in the hours leading up to training. If you get thirsty at the gym, your performance will already be suffering, so try to drink enough water in advance and then keep yourself topped up.

It is also a good idea to eat a light meal including some carbohydrates a couple of hours before training. This will make sure your muscles have the fuel they need to recover between sets.

If you are going to eat simple carbs such as sugar (see chapter 18), the ideal time is just before or during a training session. These provide fuel rapidly to the muscles. Providing you use it, the body will not turn it into fat.

Some lifters find that consuming some caffeine before training helps them and there is plenty of evidence that caffeine helps with strength exercises. One of the ways that caffeine is often taken is as part of a 'pre-workout' supplement, where it is combined with other mild stimulants and other ingredients such as beta alanine and taurine. Be careful with pre-workouts – they can include extremely high doses of their ingredients. Overstimulating the central nervous system with high doses of caffeine can make it harder to focus on good technique. Too much beta alanine can lead to strange pins-and-needles sensations, which can be off-putting. Our advice would be to avoid pre-workouts until you need them.

In the next chapter, we look at nutrition and supplements in more detail.

GENERAL WARM-UP

Before picking up a bar and starting on technical work, it is important to get yourself warmed up. This process tends to be different for each lifter, especially for those with more experience – each lifter has their own mobility challenges that they will address during their warm-up. However, there are some common things that are included.

Many lifters find that doing some light cardio to raise their heart rate at the start of a session is helpful. However, this is by no means universal – some lifters will only do this if they are feeling particularly cold or immobile.

Dynamic joint mobilisation is used as part of almost all warm-ups. Some examples are:

- Neck rotations
- Wrist rotations
- Elbow rotations
- Shoulder rotations
- Chest movements
- Side bends
- Torso rotations
- Hip hinging
- Hip rotations
- High kicks
- Leg rotations
- Knee rotations.

Foam rolling is a very popular way to mobilise as part of the warm-up. See chapter 3 for details.

There is a fair bit of evidence that stretching muscles before strength exercises actually negatively impacts performance. However, weightlifting is not all about strength and stretching can be a good way to mobilise tight muscles. Some common stretches used in warm-ups include:

- Quad stretches
- Calf stretches
- Ankle stretches
- Lunges
- Squat stretches.

See chapter 3 for more information about these stretches.

SPECIFIC WARM-UP

It is important to warm up correctly for each technical exercise that you do – just throwing weight onto the bar straightaway is not the best way to get good reps in.

Start with a bar warm-up. Like the general warm-up, each lifter will typically develop their own process for this based on their needs but a good starting point is to follow the progressions that we used in earlier chapters to learn the lifts.

For snatch:

- Snatch grip press
- Overhead squat (pause at the bottom position)
- Snatch balance
- Hip snatch
- Hang snatch.

You may also want to include Sots press (see chapter 9).

For the clean:

- Front squat (pause at the bottom position)
- Hang clean pull
- Hang clean.

It is also a good idea to do some exercises to mobilise for the rack position (see chapter 3).

For the split jerk:

- Strict press
- Press in split position
- Pop and catch in split position.

For the squat jerk:

- Strict press

- Narrow grip overhead squat.

Since the mobility requirements for the squat jerk are so tight, you will probably need to spend some extra time on stretching or foam rolling on any area that might limit you.

TECHNICAL EXERCISES

Once you have warmed up, the next part of the session will most likely focus on the Olympic lifts or their variations. More advanced lifters will sometimes do some strength work before technical exercises, but for beginners it is best to do the technical stuff before you get tired.

The key to developing really good technique is the quality of the reps you perform. There is no point doing hundreds of reps with bad form – all you are doing is drilling your body to use a bad movement pattern which will then have to be relearned later. You need to be working at a weight that is challenging but enables you to execute a really high-quality movement.

ASSISTANCE EXERCISES

After the technical part of the session, usually one or more assistance exercises are included. These will typically be squats, pulls, deadlifts or presses. As you develop as a lifter, these will be programmed specifically to address areas where you need to get stronger. As a beginner, you will probably be doing a bit of everything.

Just because these are not as technical as the Olympic lifts, don't think that you can approach them casually. Good form is still vital to get the most out of them and to avoid any risk of injury.

CORE AND CONDITIONING

Many sessions will finish with some exercises that are performed with light weights or just bodyweight. These tend to focus on general conditioning, core strength and the smaller muscles that are important for stabilising us during heavier lifts.

See chapter 11 for details of these kinds of exercises.

STRETCHING

Some people think that stretching after exercise will help to reduce the dreaded Delayed Onset Muscle Soreness (DOMS) but the evidence for this is not compelling. However, if you have time then the end of a training session is a good time to stretch for mobility as the muscles are already warm.

See chapter 3 for details of some stretches that you could include.

RECOVERY

After a training session, you want to do everything you can to help your body recover from it and be ready for the next one. It is actually during this recovery time that muscle tissue is created, so if you don't do the right things, you are lessening the value of your training.

It is important to keep your body hydrated. You will have lost some liquid during a training session, so drink some water immediately afterwards (around half a litre) and then keep drinking water regularly – around three litres a day is good goal.

Your body needs nutrients to grow muscle tissue and to produce the hormones that promote muscle growth, so consuming a good mix of protein, carbohydrates and fat is vital. We will look at this in more detail in the next chapter.

There is good evidence that proper sleep is crucial for optimal muscle growth. Also, as mentioned earlier, it is important to sleep well before training sessions in order to get the most out of them.

Some people like to do what is known as active recovery between training sessions. This typically consists of light cardio exercise such as cycling, walking or swimming. There is some limited evidence that this can help reduce muscle soreness and with feeling recovered more quickly. It certainly won't do any harm.

FOLLOWING A PROGRAMME

For your first few weeks and even months of learning the Olympic lifts and assistance exercises, you can get away without a programme. You can just turn up to the gym a few times a week and practise, adding some weight to the bar in small increments as you get more confident. This is because the weight you will be using will be low enough that you will be able to fully recover between sessions even without anything to guide you other than what you think you can lift.

If you continue to train without a plan, however, you will soon find that your progress slows and eventually stops. Beyond the absolute beginner stage, you will need to regulate your training to ensure that you can recover adequately between sessions and do not accumulate fatigue to the point that your training is negatively impacted. This kind of planning is called periodisation.

Following a programme also makes sure that you are doing enough work. Without a plan, it can sometimes be tempting to put in less effort, especially if you are not feeling great. It's amazing how much you can actually get done if you try and a written programme can help to keep you on track.

HOW TO READ A PROGRAMME

Almost all programmes are written using a sets x reps format. For example, 4x3 would mean you should do four sets of three reps each of that exercise.

Weights to use may be given in kilograms but this is usually only done when a coach has written a programme specifically for you. Most programmes are designed so that they can be adjusted to the relative strength of the lifter.

The most common way to set weights is with percentages. These always refer to your one rep maximum for that exercise. So, if your best ever snatch is 40kg and the programme says 2x3@80%, you should be doing two sets of three reps each with 32kg.

Most exercises will be performed in the 70% - 85% range.

Another way to set weights is with 'perceived exertion'. This relies on your own perception of how hard each set is to perform. There are various scales that can be used but they all boil down to thinking about how many reps you think you can do with the weight. So, the programme might say to back squat 2x3@5RM, which would mean you should squat two sets of three reps using a weight that you could do four reps with. If your coach is using this kind of system, make sure you are clear on what they want you to do.

Assistance exercises such as pulls and deadlifts are usually programmed relative to your 1RM in the exercise they are intended to support. So snatch pulls are usually based on a percentage of the snatch, clean grip deadlifts are based on your best clean and so on.

CHOOSING A PROGRAMME

If you have a coach then they should give you a programme to follow. If you don't have a coach, there is a huge range of programmes available online. We also provide a basic beginner's programme at the end of this book.

A good beginner's programme will focus on technique with lots of reps of the Olympic lifts and variations at between 70% and 80% of what you can lift for one rep. It should also include both front and back squats.

Beginner-level programmes do not need to be very long – at the beginning you can hit personal bests every week, so you could repeat a weekly programme for a while and make gains. As you progress, you will need a programme that includes lighter weeks, sometimes called deload weeks, to enable recovery. More advanced lifters follow even longer term programming with monthly, quarterly and even annual planning.

Whatever programme you choose, it is important to try to follow it as written! Unless you have a very good reason for changing it, don't. If you have a coach, you should only change your programme in conversation with them. The reason this is important is that you want to learn what kind of programme works for you. If you don't follow it, you will never know what results you could have got with the programme as written.

On the other hand, it is common for beginners to make the mistake of choosing a programme that is too demanding for them. This can result in a build-up of fatigue, many missed lifts and a decline in performance. It is normal for more experienced lifters to push their limit and, as a result, miss a proportion of lifts. As a beginner, you should be aiming to complete the vast majority of the lifts you attempt. If you miss more than a few, consider lowering the weights you are attempting.

Something that helps a lot of lifters to stick to their programme and gain as much information as possible about what works is to keep a detailed log of all the training that you do. Writing the weights, sets and reps of each exercise that you do in training sessions, along with some notes on how things went can be really valuable when looking back over your training.

USING STRAPS

As we mentioned in chapter 2, it can be use to use straps for some of your training. They are commonly used for snatches (and snatch variations), pulls and deadlifts.

We would recommend that you never use straps for cleans – if a clean goes wrong, you need to be able to dump the bar as quickly as possible so attaching yourself to it, no matter how loosely, is not a good idea!

The most basic straps are just a strip of tough material. Start with your less dominant hand as you will have to put the second strap on using one hand.

Wrap the strap around your wrist with the ends the same length, flipping one of the ends over.

Put the ends between your fingers.

Get your hand close to the bar and pass the ends around it.

Flip the ends over the bar, secure them under your hand and rotate your hand to pull the strap tight.

Now repeat the process for your other hand. This will be a bit trickier but with practice it becomes easy.

You can also get straps that have a loop built in to them. They are used slightly differently but you should still start with your less dominant hand.

Pass the unlooped end of the strap through the loop and put your wrist through the big loop that is formed.

Get your hand close to the bar and pass the free end of the strap around it.

Pass the end of the strap around the bar once.

Secure the strap under your hand and rotate your hand to pull the strap tight.

Whichever type of strap you use, stick to only wrapping it once around the bar. That is plenty to secure the bar while also enabling you to release it quickly if you need to.

AVOIDING INJURY

Done properly, weightlifting is a very safe sport. It has a much lower rate of injury than team sports such as football or rugby. It also has a lower incidence of injury than running. It's worth remembering, though, that moving large weights around is always going to carry some risk, so we need to do what we can to minimise that risk.

The most important way to avoid injury is to execute each and every rep of every exercise in your training with the correct form and with complete focus. Don't get distracted and start doing sloppy lifts. In particular, keeping a tight back is vital. This is just as true for assistance exercises as it is for the competition lifts. Keep your focus all the way to the end of every training session.

Secondly, you need to be realistic about what weights you attempt to lift. You need to add weight gradually, building confidence and perfecting your technique rather than piling weight onto the bar and failing too many lifts.

Assuming you are using good technique and are not overreaching, the other thing you can do to avoid injury while weightlifting is to learn how to dump a lift that is not going right. Doing a snatch and the bar passes backwards over your head? Dump it. Doing a jerk and you don't get your arms locked before you catch the bar? Dump it.

Dumping a snatch is easy. You just need to know whether to drop the bar in front of you or behind.

Most of the time, when you miss a snatch, the bar will fall in front of you, so you can just guide it down with your arms and let go of it when it is close to the platform.

Dumping a Snatch In Front

If you get the bar overhead but it moves too far backwards, you need to let go of the bar and move yourself forwards so that the bar will drop behind you.

Dumping a Snatch Behind

Dumping a clean is even easier – you just need to drop your elbows and allow the bar to drop in front of you. This will tend to happen in missed cleans without you even needing to think about it.

Dumping a jerk from overhead is easy too – if the bar is too far forward, step back and allow the bar to fall in front of you. If the bar is too far back, step forward and let go of the bar so that it drops behind you.

Assuming you don't fight to rescue lifts that are a lost cause and you dump them correctly, you should be very safe.

While a failed lift is an obvious potential cause of an injury, less obvious injuries are actually much more common. These are usually caused by overuse of joints, muscles and connecting tissue leading to inflammation. The best way to avoid this kind of injury is to mobilise well and do plenty of conditioning work (see chapters 3 and 11).

Another surprising source of injuries that are easily avoided is lack of care while loading weight on the bar. Make sure to adopt a good strong position, straddling the bar and with your back flat, while loading plates onto the sleeves.

HAND CARE

The most common type of injury for weightlifters is damage to the hands. While relatively minor, these kinds of injury are irritating and can even prevent training. Fortunately, there are some things you can do to look after your hands.

Chalk on the hands can help keep them dry during lifting, which will reduce damage. You can also use straps some of the time, especially for heavy pulls and deadlifts, to reduce the wear and tear on the hands.

If you regularly train with a barbell, your hand will develop hard calluses due to the friction from the bar knurling. These are both good and bad. Having tougher skin can be helpful but if calluses get too thick, they can tear, taking the skin with them.

As calluses start to form, it's a good idea to keep them under control with a pumice stone, nail file or, in extreme cases, some small scissors.

It is also a good idea to moisturise your hands to maintain some flexibility in the skin.

If you do tear the skin on your hands, make sure to disinfect it thoroughly and change the dressing on it regularly to help it to heal as fast as possible.

CHAPTER 18

NUTRITION

If you are going to do as well as you can in weightlifting, you will have to gain muscle. If you end up competing, you will also want to be in the lowest possible weight category, so you want to minimise fat as a percentage of your overall mass. You can train as hard as you like but, if your nutrition is not right, you won't achieve these goals.

As a beginner, no one is going to expect you to use elite-standard nutrition, which usually involves an individually tailored plan from a nutrition expert. This chapter is too short to cover everything but there are some simple things you can do to make sure your body is getting what it needs to get stronger and stay as lean as possible.

TRACKING NUTRITION

As with your training, keeping a log of your nutrition can help to keep you on track and enable you to see what works for you. This could be as simple as a notebook but, especially if you are looking to change your habits, a dedicated nutrition app such as MyFitnessPal can be a great way to log what you are eating in detail and track it over time against your goals.

FOOD

We usually divide the nutrition we get from food into two main groups – macronutrients that we need a lot of and micronutrients that the body needs but only in very small quantities. Macronutrients consist of protein, fat and carbohydrates. Micronutrients include vitamins and minerals.

Protein

The most obvious thing that you want to make sure you are eating plenty of is protein – the basic building material of muscles.

Plenty of research has been done on the amount of protein that is needed to maximise the gains from strength training. There isn't any completely settled answer and this is definitely something that varies from person to person. Most evidence shows that 2.2g of protein per kg of body mass is definitely enough. If you have a little bit more protein than your body needs, it is just excreted with no harmful effects, so there's no evidence for any harm in maintaining this level, provided you don't have a medical condition.

Protein is not all the same. Different protein sources have different proportions of the amino acids – the building blocks that make up proteins. In order to ensure that you are getting a good mix of amino acids, you need some variety in the meats, fish or vegetable protein that you eat.

Fat

Thankfully the myth that fat should be avoided at all costs has largely been dispelled. Fats are important to the body for the production of hormones such as testosterone, which is key to building muscles.

Carbohydrates

Carbohydrates provide the fuel that makes muscles work and so a healthy carb intake is important for maximising your training. However, too many carbohydrates can lead to gaining fat.

Carbohydrates are typically divided into two broad categories. Simple carbohydrates, such as sugar, are processed by the body very quickly and lead to a rapid spike in blood sugar. Complex carbohydrates, like those in starchy foods such as potatoes or pasta, take longer to process and so are used by the body over a longer period of time.

In general, you want the majority of the carbohydrates that you eat to be complex.

Fibre

Fibre is the parts of food that the body does not completely digest. Although the body does not make direct use of it, it is still an important part of what we eat. Fibre aids the digestion of other nutrients and there is plenty of evidence that a good fibre intake has a range of health benefits, including reduced risk of a number of diseases.

Fibre mainly comes from plant-based foods, especially beans, whole grains, vegetables, some fruits (especially the skins), nuts and seeds

Micronutrients

Micronutrients are all of the substances that the body needs that do not fall into one of the macronutrient categories. Most micronutrients are either vitamins or minerals. Vitamins are organic compounds which the body cannot produce itself, or cannot produce enough of on its own. Minerals are elements that plants and animals cannot produce at all – they must work their way up the food chain from soil to plants and eventually into animals.

Different foods contain different quantities of micronutrients so the key is to eat a varied diet and maybe supplement with vitamin and mineral pills.

WATER

Water is vital for almost every process in the human body, so it's important to make sure that you are adequately hydrated.

You can actually get quite a lot of water from the foods that you eat but, especially if you are going to be training hard, you will need to drink some water as well.

The amount of water we need varies a lot from person to person. Age, body weight, sex, activity levels and temperature all affect the required amount. The amount and type of food we eat will determine how much water we are getting in it. So, while there are some guidelines for how much water you should drink, you really need to find what works for you.

When the water content of the body drops below a certain level, the thirst instinct kicks in to prompt us to increase our water intake by drinking. So, if you want to optimise your hydration levels, you should aim to be drinking enough that you don't get thirsty. Don't go crazy though – drinking excessive quantities of water can cause low sodium levels in the blood, which can be dangerous.

SUPPLEMENTS

In an ideal world, we would get all of our nutritional needs from a balanced diet of healthy foods and we wouldn't need to use supplements. The reality for many of us is that supplementation is a useful way to make sure we are getting enough of everything we need.

There is a bewildering array of supplements available and we don't have the space to cover everything here, so we'll look at the main things that are in supplements that weightlifters often use.

Protein

If you don't think you are getting enough protein in your food, protein supplementation has been shown to be effective. Consuming protein in this form can also be very cost effective if budget is an issue.

Studies have found no harmful effects of protein supplementation in healthy people.

Whey protein is the most commonly used type of protein. It contains a good mix of amino acids and is relatively cheap. This kind of protein is digested quickly by the body, so is good for immediately after a training session.

Like whey, casein comes from milk and contains a complete range of amino acids but is digested more slowly by the body. This makes it good for maintaining the level of amino acids in the body over a period of time, such as overnight.

Since whey and casein are from milk, some people are allergic to them and must seek out other protein sources. Egg protein can be an option (although some people are allergic to eggs) but is expensive.

For vegans, there are options based on soy, rice, hemp and peas. The weakness of these options is that often they do not include all of the required amino acids and so must be combined with other protein or amino acid sourced in order to give you what you need.

Branched Chain Amino Acids (BCAAs)

As we mentioned earlier, proteins we consume are broken down in the body into amino acids before being recombined into the proteins we need to build muscle.

There is now a whole range of supplements that include the amino acids themselves. This skips the requirement for the body to break down source proteins, meaning that the amino acids are available more quickly.

Since the body needs a wide range of different BCAAs, a good rule of thumb is to opt for supplements that contain a range of different BCAAs rather than just a small selection.

Creatine

Creatine is a compound that is produced naturally in the body and is also consumed in meat and fish. It has an important role in how the muscles produce energy during exercise. Many combined supplements include creatine as an ingredient.

There is good evidence that raising creatine levels through supplementation can give benefits during training. While it won't directly make you stronger, it does seem to help with training more at a higher intensity.

The evidence shows that between 4g and 10g per day should be used in order to get the benefits of creatine supplementation.

Some people do experience some side effects of creatine supplementation. Water retention is the most common, leading to a slight weight gain which is lost as soon as supplementation ends. Minor digestive issues and cramps have also been reported but are not widespread.

Beta Alanine

Beta alanine is an amino acid that is not used to build muscle protein. Instead, it is used in the production of carnosine, which helps prevent lactic acid build-up during exercise. Lactic acid is an unwanted by-product of the energy systems used by muscles and is what results in the 'burn' of intense exercise.

Most studies have found that long-term beta alanine supplementation is required in order to get the benefits. Between 15g and 30g a week over several weeks has been shown to increase carnosine levels.

If you consume too much beta alanine at once then you can experience a rather disconcerting tingling sensation called parasthesia, so it is best to use a small amount at a time.

Vitamins

While you should be getting all the vitamins you need from your food, it is cheap and easy to take a multivitamin each day to ensure you are getting what you need, so many weightlifters do this.

CAFFEINE

Caffeine is the world's most widely used stimulant, both in the general population and among weightlifters. There is good evidence that the stimulation it gives to the central nervous system can help with intense training.

If you ingest lots of caffeine, the body will develop a tolerance to it. This means that, over time, you will get less benefit from the same amount of caffeine. This leads to many people increasing their intake, only to become tolerant to progressively higher amounts of caffeine. In order to reset your sensitivity, you need to stop taking caffeine completely for a couple of weeks and then use as little caffeine as required to get the benefits you want.

ALCOHOL

Unlike the other things in this chapter, alcohol is something that is pretty clearly a negative for weightlifting performance in anything more than very small amounts. We all have to decide what we are prepared to sacrifice in order to make progress in our lifting. Obviously this decision is very different for an elite athlete compared to a recreational lifter but it's still important for us all to be aware of how drinking is likely to affect our training.

We're not going to be talking about the well-known negative effects of drinking too much alcohol in the long term – we're just focused on the short-term consequences of a drinking session on training.

It's also important to recognise that social drinking, in moderation, can have a positive aspect. A bit of relaxation away from training can be important and many people do find that having a few drinks helps with that.

Alcohol and Muscle Growth

There is plenty of evidence that drinking more than a small amount of alcohol reduces muscle growth for a period afterwards. Without getting into the details of the science, it seems that alcohol in the body impacts the processes that our body uses to recover between training sessions. This is obviously not good if you are working hard on a training programme to get stronger.

What counts as a small amount? Many of the studies have found that the biggest effects kick in when consuming around 0.5g to 1g of alcohol per kg of body weight. So, as a rule of thumb, you shouldn't drink more alcohol in grams than your body weight in kg. Ideally, you want to limit yourself to around half of that.

Here's a handy table showing some popular drinks and how much alcohol they contain:

Drink	Alcohol Content (g)
Beer (4%) - pint	18
Beer (5%) - small bottle (12oz/330ml)	13
Wine (12%) - small glass (4.5oz / 125ml)	14
Wine (12%) - medium glass (6oz / 175ml)	20
Wine (12%) - large glass (9oz / 250ml)	28
Spirit (37.5%) - single (25ml / 1oz)	8
Spirit (37.5%) - double (50ml / 2oz)	16

So a lifter with a body weight of 90kg is going to start running into the effects seen in studies at around three pints while for a lifter weighing 65kg it will be two pints. Drinking twice that amount is going to put you in the zone where you experience strong negative effects. Watch out for large glasses of wine – even a couple of glasses are going to put smaller lifters into the zone where training will start to be impacted!

It is worth noting that everyone's body is going to respond differently to alcohol, so the 1g/kg of body weight idea is not going to work perfectly for everyone. If you want to be sure, you will have to drink less or even avoid alcohol completely.

Studies have shown that the negative effects of alcohol can persist for up to sixty hours or more, with higher amounts of alcohol having longer-lasting effects. Having said that, there is no evidence for infrequent drinking sessions having long-term negative effects on training, so if you have a few days off over Christmas, drinking a bit more than recommended above is not going to ruin training for January.

Alcohol and Body Fat

Alcohol is a poison and your body treats it as such. That means that the body will use it ahead of other sources of calories in order to get it out of the body as quickly as possible. The problem here is not so much that the alcohol will get turned into fat (it's possible but difficult) but rather that, while the body is busy with the alcohol, it is not using carbohydrates or fat as a fuel source. This is especially a problem if you eat high-carb foods while drinking. Even worse are drinks that combine alcohol and sugars – the sugars will just get turned into fat as the alcohol is used.

If you want to minimise the carbs in what you drink, the website Get Drunk Not Fat provides details on the alcohol:calories ratio for many popular drinks.

A potentially bigger effect of alcohol on body fat is the tendency that many people have to eat more when they are drinking and to eat foods that are more likely to lead to gaining fat. This effect has been studied and is very real, although it does not affect everyone to the same extent. One way to work around this effect is to have some high-protein snacks available to eat during or after drinking, in order to avoid more high-carb options.

Hangovers

In weightlifting, technique training is arguably even more important than muscle growth, at least for beginners. Clearly, carrying a fuzzy head from the night before and being heavily dehydrated is not going to be a good recipe for training technical lifts.

The hangover from moderate drinking is only going to last a day so the best approach may be to plan social drinking when the following day is a rest day. If that is not possible then drinking needs to be limited and you need to drink plenty of water during the evening, before going to bed and in the morning. It is also a good idea to get some sodium and potassium in – rehydration treatments such as Dioralyte are an easy way to replace lost salts.

What to do?

So, what's the takeaway from all of this? Obviously, the absolute best thing to do in terms of training and performance is to not drink at all, but there are things you can do to ensure some social drinking doesn't have a significant impact on your lifting. Here's our advice:

- Keep drinking in moderation, limited to the equivalent of three or four pints of beer or even less for smaller lifters
- Try to plan your socialising and training to avoid training the day after a drinking session
- Rehydrate after drinking with plenty of water and, if possible, rehydration salts
- Expect to gain some body fat if you drink with food and plan accordingly.

CHAPTER 19

DEVELOPING AS A LIFTER

I n this book, we have established the foundations you need to get started in Olympic weightlifting. What comes next is a lifetime of striving to get better and hit progressively bigger personal bests.

In this chapter we will look at what lies ahead.

MAKING AND MEASURING PROGRESS

A nice thing about weightlifting is that there is an easy way to measure your progress by the weights you are able to lift. Many weightlifters find it valuable to keep a log of their lifting so that they can see how week by week and month by month their commitment to training turns into progressively bigger lifts.

The key to long term success in weightlifting is steady, sustainable progress. It is much better to make continual small improvements to your personal bests over a period of years than to make big gains and then stop training properly for a period and lose some of them.

IMPROVING TECHNIQUE

As a beginner, you should be focusing on technique ahead of putting more weight on the bar. That's not to say that you shouldn't challenge yourself – sometimes technical flaws aren't apparent when the weight is too light. Just make sure that you are practising at a weight where you can use a good movement pattern.

The consensus is that beginner lifters benefit from doing most of their training with 70%-85% of their best lifts. This is heavy enough to be a challenge but light enough to enable the best possible technique to be used.

As a beginner, you will probably not know what your one-rep maximums are. A good guide is to aim to feel like you would be able to perform one more rep with good form after the end of each set. That way, you will be working at a weight that is enough below your maximum that you should be able to use your best form.

Doing lots of reps with a good movement pattern is important for making completing lifts this way second nature. This is often referred to as 'muscle memory' but actually has more to do with the central nervous system. By practising with lighter weights, we hope to make the movements instinctive so that, even with heavier weights, we will always use an efficient technique.

Right at the start, you will probably find that technique improvement will lead to frequent, significant jumps in the weights you can lift in the Olympic weightlifting movements. This will be especially true if you are also making mobility improvements. Over time, you will find that these jumps become smaller and less frequent. You may even have frustrating periods where you seem to be going backwards.

When you change something in your technique, you may find that things seem to get worse for a while. Because you are doing something unfamiliar, lifts can feel heavier and you may have to use lighter weights and build back up to your previous best lifts.

The Powerful Ideas Press book *Improve at Olympic Weightlifting* includes a wealth of additional information on how to identify and correct technical problems with your lifts.

GETTING STRONGER

For most people, gaining strength is a much steadier process than improving technique, provided they put the required work in. Beginners still make the most rapid gains but even experienced lifters can get stronger at a relatively predictable rate.

The Powerful Ideas Press book *Improve at Olympic Weightlifting* includes a complete coverage of strength training for intermediate and advanced lifters.

COMPETING

While you can do Olympic weightlifting just for fun, it is at heart a competitive sport. If you never compete, you will be missing out on a lot of what makes weightlifting so rewarding.

Even if you have no desire to be competitive in the sense of beating other lifters, competitions are a great place to test yourself. It's one thing to make a lift in the gym but to get a personal best in front of three referees proves it was definitely a good lift.

Competitions are also brilliant for giving you something to focus on during training programmes. If you know you have a competition coming up, you are much more likely to commit to making all of you training sessions count.

When should you compete?

Compete as soon as you feel ready. Local open competitions have no qualification standards. As long as you can lift the bar plus light plates and competition collars (usually a total of 30kg for woman and 35kg for men), you can start competing.

A common mistake is for lifters to think they need to reach a certain standard before they start competing. In fact, competing can actually help you to raise your standard more quickly and, if you want to compete seriously in the future, the more experience you can gain of the competition environment the better.

Competitions are divided into weight categories but don't worry about this to start with – you can just compete in whichever weight category you are in. Your priority for your first few competitions should just be to make good lifts and progress from one competition to the next. There will be plenty of time in the future to worry about placings and qualifying for national or even international competition.

Older lifters (thirty-five and up) can compete in masters competitions, which are divided into age as well as weight categories. This creates a more level playing field for everyone.

What happens at a competition?

At a competition, you get to have three attempts at snatches and three at clean and jerks.

Competition day starts with weigh-in, usually two hours before you actually compete. The time of the weigh-in will depend on which session you are in – there may be several sessions in a single competition day. At this point you have to let the organisers know what you plan to lift for your first snatch and your first clean and jerk.

After weigh-in, you get a bit of a break where you can eat and drink liquids – this becomes more important for more experienced lifters, who may have needed to drop some weight to get into their chosen weight category.

Most lifters start to warm up about half an hour before they will do their first competition lift. There is a dedicated area at the competition for this, usually called the warm-up room. This warm-up is much like what you would do at the start of a training session. The key thing is to time it correctly so that you will be ready at the right time for your first lift on the competition platform.

Ten minutes before the session starts, the lifters are presented to the audience. This will fall during the warm-ups of at least some of the lifters.

The session itself starts with the snatch. A 'rising bar' format is used where the lifter who announced the lowest starting weight is called to the platform first, followed by the next heaviest and so on. Each lifter gets a minute from when they are called to the platform to make their attempt.

Lifters or their coaches have a number of chances to adjust their attempts, which can lead to the order changing. This is the source of many tactics that are used at national and international competitions.

When a lifter makes an attempt, three referees watch and adjudge it either a 'good lift' or a 'no lift', usually with a white light for 'good lift' or a red light for 'no lift'. You need at least two referees to declare a lift good to be awarded the lift. There are several rules about what you are allowed to do during the lifts but the most common thing that referees fail a seemingly successful lift for is a press-out. This is when the bar is not caught overhead with locked arms but rather pressed into position.

Once all of the lifters have had three attempts at the snatch, there is sometimes a short break before the whole process is repeated again for the clean and jerk.

The winner of each weight category is decided by the total of each lifter's best snatch and best clean and jerk. If there is a draw, the lifter who got the total first is the winner.

The Powerful Ideas Press book *Compete in Olympic Weightlifting* includes full coverage of how to prepare for competitions, what happens on the day and how to get the best possible results.

APPENDIX ONE - GLOSSARY

Weightlifting comes with a lot of specialised terms that can get confusing until you are used to them. Hopefully this glossary will help with making sense of what coaches and lifter are talking about!

1RM - One Rep Max - The amount of weight a lifter can perform a single repetition of a movement with. Other rep maxes are sometimes used as well (e.g. 3RM or 5RM)

Anterior Chain - The muscles on the front of your body

Barbell/Bar – A metal bar with sleeves at the ends designed for carrying weight plates and with knurling for grip.

Block – A sturdy box that is used to raise the bar to a particular height for certain exercises.

Bodybuilding – Training to achieve an aesthetically pleasing physique.

Bumper – see Plate.

Catch – The position in a weightlifting movement where the lifter locks their arms out with the bar overhead.

Clean – An exercise where a barbell is lifted from the floor to shoulder height in one movement.

Clean and jerk – An exercise where a barbell is lifted from the floor to above the head in two movements: the clean, which brings the bar to the shoulders; and the jerk, which moves it above the head. The combined exercise is one of the weightlifting competition lifts.

Clean grip – Holding the bar with the hands just wide enough that they are clear of the legs during the exercise.

Collar – A locking device the holds the plates onto the barbell.

Cue - A short phrase or single word used by a coach to encourage a lifter to perform a movement in a particular way.

Deficit – Any exercise carried out from an elevated position so that the bar is lower relative to the lifter than in the normal version.

Dip – A downward movement used at the start of a jerk, before the drive.

Dorsiflexion – movement at the ankles where the shins are brought closer to the toes. The opposite is plantar-flexion.

Double - A set of two reps

Drive – The explosive upward movement in the jerk, after the dip.

Drop – The phase of the snatch or clean where the lifter pulls themselves downwards under the bar into a deep squat.

First pull/First phase – The part of the snatch or clean where the bar is raised from the platform to the height of the knees.

Foam rolling – Using a hard foam cylinder to massage the muscles.

Good morning – An exercise that involves hinging at the hips to bring the shoulders forwards and down.

Halting – A variation of an exercise where the lifter stops at certain positions.

Hang – A variation of the snatch or clean that is started with the bar already partway up towards the power position.

Hook grip – A technique for gripping the bar in which the thumbs are placed under one or more of the fingers to enable a secure grip without tight arms.

Jerk – An exercise where the barbell is moved from the shoulders to above the head without pressing it with the arms.

Paused – see Halting.

PB - Personal Best - The highest weight a lifter has successfully lifted for a particular movement.

Power – A variation of a lift where the lifter does not drop so deep to catch the bar as they would in the normal version.

Plantar-flexion – Movement of the ankles that takes the shins further away from the toes. The opposite of dorsiflexion.

Plate – the weights that are added to the barbell to create the desired load for training or competition. Usually for weightlifting these are coated in rubber (bumper plates).

Platform – The surface that weightlifting is performed on.

Plyometrics – Exercises that involve using the stretch reflex of muscles, such as jumps.

Posterior Chain - The muscles down your back and the back of your legs

Power position – The position in the snatch or clean where the bar is ready to be driven upwards in the second pull.

Powerlifting – A strength sport consisting of the squat, bench press and deadlift.

Press – Any exercise where the arms are used to push the barbell from the shoulders to above the head.

Press out – Finishing a snatch or jerk by using the arms, an illegal movement in competition.

Programme – A series of specified training sessions provided by a coach for an athlete to follow.

Proprioception – The sense of where your own body is and what it is doing.

Recovery – The phase in a snatch, clean or jerk where the lifter returns to standing upright after the catch.

Rep/Repetition – A single exercise, usually part of a set of multiple reps.

Second pull – The phase of the snatch or clean where the bar is driven upwards with maximal force.

Segment – see Halting.

Self-myofacial release – see Foam rolling

Set – A group of reps of an exercise carried out without a rest between them.

Snatch – An exercise where a barbell is lifted from the floor to above the head in a single movement; one of the weightlifting competition lifts.

Snatch grip – Holding the bar with hands wide, usually so that the bar is at hip height when standing upright.

Split jerk – A style of jerk where the feet are split, with one moving forwards and one backwards to drop under and catch the bar.

Squat – Any of a number of movements that involve bending at the knees and hips to lower the torso.

Squat jerk – a style of jerk where the lifter drops into a deep squat to catch the bar.

The pull - this phrase always refers to the second pull of the snatch and clean

Transition – The part of the snatch or clean where the bar is raised from the knees to the power position.

Triple - A set of three reps

Triple Extension - A common way to refer to the extension part of the snatch and clean.

Strongman – A strength sport that uses a wide variety of events, including some taken from weightlifting and powerlifting.

Thoracic spine – The part of the spine at the level of the chest.

Weightlifting – A strength sport consisting of the snatch and the clean and jerk.

WOD – Workout Of the Day – a term used mainly in CrossFit® for a particular set of exercises carried out in sequence, usually against the clock.

APPENDIX TWO - FURTHER INFORMATION

These organisations are responsible for weightlifting in their respective countries. They organise national competitions and send teams to international events. Most of them have schemes for regulating coaching of the sport with certification systems. They are a good first point of call to find local weightlifting coaches and clubs.

These are the NGBs for the main English-speaking nations

British Weightlifting

http://britishweightlifting.org

USA Weightlifting

https://www.teamusa.org/USA-Weightlifting

Canadian Weightlifting Federation

http://www.halterophiliecanada.ca

Australian Weightlifting Federation

https://www.awf.com.au

Olympic Weightlifting New Zealand

http://olympicweightlifting.nz

PODCASTS

All of these podcasts feature a range of content, from roundups of major competitions through to advice for beginners.

Weightlifting House

https://www.weightliftinghouse.com/podcast

The Everyday Weightlifter

http://findaweightliftingcoach.com/everyday-weightlifter

Weightlifting Life

https://www.catalystathletics.com/podcast

The Sinclair Debate

https://www.facebook.com/TheSinclairDebate

Jugg Life

https://thejugglife.com

NEWS SITES AND BLOGSNEWS SITES AND BLOGS

These sites mainly focus on elite weightlifters, featuring interviews and competition results, but they also include articles that will be useful to you.

All Things Gym

https://www.allthingsgym.com/

Juggernaut

http://www.jtsstrength.com/articles/category/weightlifting/

Weightlifting House

https://www.weightliftinghouse.com/

Bar Bend

https://barbend.com/category/weightlifting/

ONLINE FORUMS

These two sites are the main places to go if you want to ask questions or just talk about weightlifting. Like all online forums, they have a mixture of participants from genuinely helpful to outright trolls.

Reddit Weightlifting

https://www.reddit.com/r/weightlifting/

WLForums

http://wlforums.com/forums/forum.php

ONLINE VIDEO CHANNELS

These two channels are the main place to go if you want to watch elite lifters, including slow-motion shots that really capture the movements.

All Things Gym

https://www.youtube.com/user/allthingsgym

Hook Grip

https://www.youtube.com/user/hookgrip

These channels include more content that will help beginner or intermediate lifters:

California Strength

https://www.youtube.com/user/CaliforniaStrength

Zack Telander

https://www.youtube.com/channel/UC94_fvLx7abZgs9LIkM7jxw

(or search for 'Zack Telander' on YouTube)

APPENDIX THREE - BEGINNERS PROGRAMMES

PROGRAM 1 - LEARNING THE LIFTS

O ur first program is designed to take you through all of the learning progressions for the snatch, clean and split jerk from earlier in the book (see chapters 5, 6 and 7)

If you do three sessions per week, this program will take you about a month to complete, by which point you will have tried the basic technique for all of the Olympic weightlifting movements.

Session 1

This is your first session of weightlifting so take things slowly. Warm up well and, don't rush through the exercises. The number of sets here is the fewest you should do - if anything doesn't feel right, do some extra sets until it does.

1. Warmup
2. Find Your Grip Width
3. Overhead Squat - 3 sets of 3
4. Slow Snatch Balance - 1 set of 3
5. Fast Snatch Balance - 3 sets of 3
6. Scarecrow Snatch - 2 sets of 3

7. Hip Snatch - 5 sets of 3

Session 2

Now you're going to build on what you did in the first session by doing some hang snatches (after working through the exercises you did last time)

1. Warmup
2. Overhead Squat - 3 sets of 3
3. Slow Snatch Balance - 1 set of 3
4. Fast Snatch Balance - 3 sets of 3
5. Scarecrow Snatch - 1 set of 3
6. Hip Snatch - 3 sets of 3
7. Hang Snatch From Above the Knee - 5 sets of 3

Session 3

This session completes the snatch learning progression.

1. Warmup
2. Overhead Squat - 3 sets of 3
3. Fast Snatch Balance - 3 sets of 3
4. Scarecrow Snatch - 1 set of 3
5. Hip Snatch - 2 sets of 3
6. Hang Snatch From Above the Knee - 3 sets of 3
7. Hang Snatch From Shins - 5 sets of 3

If this feels easy, put the lightest full size plates you have on the bar and do some of these sets as full snatches from the platform.

Session 4

There is more practice on snatch in this session but now you will also start to prepare for learning the clean.

1. Warmup
2. Overhead Squat - 3 sets of 3
3. Fast Snatch Balance - 3 sets of 3
4. Hip Snatch - 2 sets of 3

5. Hang Snatch From Above the Knee - 1 sets of 3
6. Hang Snatch From Shins - 1 set of 3
7. Snatch - 5 sets of 3
8. Find Your Clean Grip
9. Find a Comfortable Rack Position
10. Front Squat 3 sets of 3

You may well find that you need to put a bit of weight on the bar in order to be able to get the bar into a good rack position. This is fine - compared to the snatch, we can lift bigger weights in the clean, so it's not a problem to learn with a bit of weight. Don't go crazy though - keep the weight easily manageable.

Session 5

It's time to focus on the clean for a whole session now. As with the very first session, take your time and do extra sets if anything doesn't feel right.

1. Warmup
2. Find Your Clean Grip
3. Find a Comfortable Rack Position
4. Front Squat 3 sets of 3
5. Hang Clean Pull 2 sets of 3
6. Hang Power Clean - 1 set of 3
7. Hang Clean from mid-thigh 3 sets of 3
8. Hang Clean from Knee - 3 sets of 3

Session 6

We'll reintroduce the snatch again now, along with the clean. If things are going well, you may have a bit of weight on the bar for both snatch and clean now. Everything else should be with just the bar though.

1. Warmup
2. Overhead Squat - 2 sets of 3
3. Fast Snatch Balance - 2 sets of 3
4. Hip Snatch - 1 sets of 3
5. Hang Snatch From Above the Knee - 1 sets of 3
6. Hang Snatch From Shins - 1 set of 3

7. Snatch - 3 sets of 3
8. Front Squat 2 sets of 3
9. Hang Clean Pull 1 set of 3
10. Hang Power Clean - 1 set of 3
11. Hang Clean from mid-thigh - 1 set of 3
12. Hang Clean from Knee - 1 set of 3
13. Full Clean - 5 sets of 3

Session 7

This session is all about drilling what you have done in the previous sessions. Keep your focus on hitting the right positions.

1. Warmup
2. Overhead Squat - 2 sets of 3
3. Fast Snatch Balance - 2 sets of 3
4. Hip Snatch - 1 sets of 3
5. Hang Snatch From Above the Knee - 1 sets of 3
6. Hang Snatch From Shins - 1 set of 3
7. Snatch - 3 sets of 3
8. Front Squat 2 sets of 3
9. Hang Clean from mid-thigh - 1 set of 3
10. Hang Clean from Knee - 1 set of 3
11. Full Clean - 5 sets of 3

Session 8

Now it's time to try the split jerk. As with the other movements, do extra sets if you feel like you need extra work on anything.

1. Warmup
2. Choose your Split Jerk Front Foot
3. Split Position
4. Splits without the Bar - 3 sets of 3
5. Overhead Press in Split Position - 2 sets of 5
6. Dip Drive and Catch in Split Position - 2 sets of 3
7. Jerk Recovery - 1 set of 3
8. Standing Dip, Drive and Catch - 2 sets of 3

9. Split Jerk - 5 sets of 3

Session 9

You have now tried all of the movements so the next couple of sessions consist of drilling what you have done. The clean and jerk are still separate at this point.

1. Warmup
2. Overhead Squat - 2 sets of 3
3. Fast Snatch Balance - 2 sets of 3
4. Hip Snatch - 1 sets of 3
5. Hang Snatch From Above the Knee - 1 sets of 3
6. Hang Snatch From Shins - 1 set of 3
7. Snatch - 3 sets of 3
8. Front Squat 2 sets of 3
9. Hang Clean from mid-thigh - 1 set of 3
10. Hang Clean from Knee - 1 set of 3
11. Full Clean - 5 sets of 3
12. Splits without the Bar - 1 set of 3
13. Overhead Press in Split Position - 1 set of 5
14. Dip Drive and Catch in Split Position - 1 sets of 3
15. Split Jerk - 5 sets of 3

Session 10

This is your last session before putting the clean and jerk together.

1. Warmup
2. Overhead Squat - 2 sets of 3
3. Fast Snatch Balance - 2 sets of 3
4. Hip Snatch - 1 sets of 3
5. Hang Snatch From Above the Knee - 1 sets of 3
6. Hang Snatch From Shins - 1 set of 3
7. Snatch - 3 sets of 3
8. Front Squat 2 sets of 3
9. Hang Clean from mid-thigh - 1 set of 3
10. Hang Clean from Knee - 1 set of 3

11. Full Clean - 5 sets of 3
12. Splits without the Bar - 1 set of 3
13. Overhead Press in Split Position - 1 set of 5
14. Dip Drive and Catch in Split Position - 1 sets of 3
15. Split Jerk - 5 sets of 3

Session 11

Now its time to combine the clean and jerk

1. Warmup
2. Overhead Squat - 2 sets of 3
3. Fast Snatch Balance - 2 sets of 3
4. Hip Snatch - 1 sets of 3
5. Hang Snatch From Above the Knee - 1 sets of 3
6. Hang Snatch From Shins - 1 set of 3
7. Snatch - 3 sets of 3
8. Front Squat 2 sets of 3
9. Overhead Press in Split Position - 1 set of 5
10. Dip Drive and Catch in Split Position - 1 set of 3
11. Hang Clean and Split Jerk - 2 sets of 3
12. Clean and Jerk - 5 sets of 3

Session 12

This is the last session of the learning progression. Now is the time to try putting a bit more weight on the bar. The sets for snatch and clean and jerk are doubles rather than triples, so you can try adding a bit more weight. For most people, 5kg is the most you will want to add between sets at this stage.

1. Warmup
2. Overhead Squat - 2 sets of 3
3. Fast Snatch Balance - 2 sets of 3
4. Hip Snatch - 1 set of 3
5. Hang Snatch From Above the Knee - 1 set of 3
6. Hang Snatch From Shins - 1 set of 3
7. Snatch - 5 sets of 2

8. Front Squat 2 sets of 3
9. Overhead Press in Split Position - 1 set of 5
10. Dip Drive and Catch in Split Position - 1 sets of 3
11. Hang Clean and Split Jerk - 2 sets of 3
12. Clean and Jerk - 5 sets of 2

PROGRAM TWO - PRACTICE MAKES PERFECT

This program consists of a series of exercises you can perform using just the bar, concentrating on technique and speed.

These circuits of exercises are also great for using as a warmup for other programs. You could also do these sessions on rest days for extra technique practise once you start adding weight in your main training sessions.

Each session of this program consists of the following exercises with a short rest between each circuit.

3 circuits of:

- 5 overhead squats
- 5 presses from the back of the neck (snatch grip)
- 5 snatch balance

6 circuits of:

- 2 hip snatches
- 2 hang snatches
- 2 full snatches

2 circuits of:

- 10 front squats
- 10 clean grip deadlifts

6 circuits of:

- 2 hang clean from mid thigh
- 2 hang cleans from above the knee

- 2 full cleans

6 circuits of:

- 3 shoulder presses
- 3 push presses
- 3 power jerks
- 3 split jerks

PROGRAM THREE - FOUR WEEK PROGRAM

This program is designed for use once you feel like you have a decent technique and are ready to start adding some weight to the bar. It is designed to lead to new PBs every four weeks.

Week 1 Day 1

Snatch

- 70%/ 5 5 4
- 80%/ 4 4
- 85%/ 3 3

Snatch Pulls

- 60%/ 5 5 5
- 70%/ 4 4 4

Back squat

- 70%/ 5 5 5
- 80%/ 4 4 4

Week 1 Day 2

Clean

- 70%/ 5 5 4

- 80%/ 4 4
- 85%/ 3 3

Front squat

- 70%/ 5 5 5
- 80%/ 4 4 4

Clip Grip Deadlift

- 70%/ 5 5 5
- 80%/ 4 4 4

Week 1 Day 3

Jerk

- 70%/ 4 4 4
- 80%/ 3 3 3

Clean grip pulls

- 90%/ 5 5 5
- 100%/ 4 4 4

Shoulder press

- 70%/ 5 5 5 5 5

Week 2 Day 1

Snatch

- 80%/ 4 4 3
- 85%/ 3 3
- 90%/ 2 2

Snatch grip pulls

- 100%/ 4 4 4
- 110%/ 3 3 3

Back squat

- 80%/ 4 4 4
- 85%/ 3 3 3

Week 2 Day 2

Clean

- 80%/ 4 4 3
- 85%/ 3 3
- 90%/ 2 2

Front squat

- 80%/ 4 4 4
- 85%/ 3 3 3

Deadlift

- 80%/ 4 4 4
- 85%/ 3 3 3

Week 2 Day 3

Jerk

- 80%/ 3 3 3
- 85%/ 2 2 2

Overhead squat with clean grip

- 5 sets of 5 reps

(focus on positioning not on weight)

Strict press

- 75%/ 5 5 5
- 80%/ 4 4 4

Week 3 Day 1

Snatch

- 85%/ 3 3 2
- 90%/ 2 2
- +90%/ 2 2

Snatch grip pulls

- 100%/ 3 3 3
- 110%/ 2 2 2

Back squat

- 85%/ 3 3 3
- 90%/ 2 2

Week 3 Day 2

Clean & Jerk

- 85%/ 2+2 2+2
- 90%/ 2+1 1+2
- 95%/ 1+1 1+1

Deadlift

- 85%/ 3 3 3
- 90%/ 2 2 2

Week 3 Day 3

Front squat

- 85%/ 3 3 3
- 90%/ 2 2

Push press

- 85%/ 5 5 5
- 90%/ 4 4 4

Week 4 Day 1

Snatch

- 85%/ 2 2 2
- 90%/ 2
- 95%/ 2
- 100%/ 1
- +100%/ 1

Back squat

- 85%/ 3 3
- 90%/ 2 2

Week 4 Day 2

Deadlift

- 85%/ 3 3
- 90%/ 2 2

Push press

- 85%/ 3 3 2
- 90%/ 2 2

Week 4 Day 3

Clean & Jerk

- 85%/ 1+2 1+2
- 90%/   1+1
- 95%/   1+1
- 100%/   1+1
- +100%/   1+1

Front squat

- 85%/ 3 3
- 90%/ 2 2

INDEX

Athlete 3-4, 20, 61-62, 83, 165, 175, 199, 211

B

Background 25, 118

Balance 9, 34, 56, 63, 66-67, 75-76, 78, 87, 93-94, 103-104, 106, 109-110, 137, 181, 196, 219-225

Band 122

Barbell 4-6, 11-14, 16, 18, 49, 62, 65, 117-119, 135, 147, 150, 176, 192, 209-212

Bath 38

Battery-powered 39

BCAAs 197

Beer 202

Belt 17

Bench 5, 27, 30, 39, 46, 211

Beta Alanine 179, 197-198

Block 14, 18, 41, 43, 46, 72, 82, 91, 99, 110, 141-142, 144, 163, 165-166, 170-171, 194, 209

BLOGS 217

branched chain amino acids (see: BCAAs)

Breathing 56, 120-121, 130, 132

Broomstick 33-34, 41, 50

bumper plates 13-15, 209, 211

Bushings 12

C

Caffeine 179, 198

Cage (see: power cage)

Calf 48-49, 180

Calluses 192

Calories 201

Camera 56

Carb 179, 183, 194-195, 201

Cardio 180, 183

Carnosine 198

Casein 196

Catch 9, 25, 27, 62-63, 68, 76-77, 79-80, 83-89, 91, 95-98, 101-103, 106-111, 113-114, 118, 120, 155-159, 181, 190, 209, 211-212, 222-225

Categories 6, 25, 193-195, 205-207, 217

Caving 98

Certificates 20, 215

Chalk 16-17, 169, 192

Champion 6, 142

Chest 30-31, 68, 120, 137, 140, 180, 213

Clean 4-7, 9, 17-18, 25-27, 44, 55, 62, 83-99, 101-102, 110-111, 117-118, 123, 130, 138-142, 155, 157-161, 164-165, 168, 181, 185-186, 191, 206-207, 209-213, 219-229, 231

Clothes 16

Club 10, 20, 176, 215

Coach 4-5, 9-10, 19-21, 63, 81-82, 84, 98, 121, 162-163, 165, 177-178, 184-185, 206, 209-211, 215

Also from Powerful Ideas Press

Lightning Source UK Ltd.
Milton Keynes UK
UKHW021444141118
332336UK00006B/329/P